Here Comes The Purple Island

HERE COMES THE PURPLE ISLAND

A Story of Cultural and Artistic Administration in the Age of Population Extinction

Kim Byoung Hee and Hong Kyung Soo
Translated by **Kim Beom Joo**

HAKJISA

Preface

Awaiting Homo Viator

Scholars have illuminated various aspects of human nature. Definitions such as the thinking person (homo sapiens), the tool-using person (homo faber), or the playful person (homo ludens) have been familiar descriptions of us so far. However, the French existentialist philosopher Gabriel Marcel (1889~1973) paid special attention to the existential nature of people who cannot settle down and are constantly on the move. Interestingly, he defined human beings as 'Homo viator' (travelling people). This means that humans have an inherent instinct to move, confirming their existence in the process of departing somewhere, and travel can be seen as the pinnacle of this instinct.

We are all close to homo viator. A person might be a

traveler on a wandering path throughout their life. St. Teresa of the Middle Ages left us with the precious saying that life on earth is nothing more than "a night at a strange inn." In sculptures like Alberto Giacometti's "Walking Man" and in poems like Yoon Dong-ju's "The Road," Kim Gi-rim's "The Road," Do Jong-hwan's "The Road I Could Not Avoid," and Yoon Seok-gu's "The Road of Aging," humans are depicted as wandering travelers on a road. Singer Kang Su-ji also sang in "Violet Fragrance," "Your figure approached like a violet. I couldn't forget the fragrance in your beautiful eyes. ··· Among the many people I meet on the street, you were the one who handed me love." This is a song confessing that the person she encountered on the road handed her a violet-colored love.

How will travel evolve in the future? While this book introduces various attractions and activities in Shinan county, it is by no means a travel guide. It is a record of administrative innovation, looking back on how efforts have been made to invigorate the islands, including 74 inhabited islands and a total of 1,025 islands (commonly referred to as 1,004 islands), which make up the heaven of islands in Shinan county, Jeollanam-do, facing population cliffs and aging phenomena, based on the local environment and culture. Various local autonomous entities have carried out administration for regional regeneration, but innovative examples such as the color marketing of Purple island in Shinan county are rare. It is even more meaningful as a result of the administrative leaders, members, and residents practicing change and innovation together. The authors joined forces with the intention of overcoming the limitations of existing regional regeneration reports or tourist guidebooks. Based on this awareness of the problem, two people co-authored the book "Here Comes The Purple Island: A Story of Cultural and Artistic Administration in the Age of Population Extinction," which is now being released to the world. If I briefly introduce the contents of this book, which is composed of four chapters, it would be as follows.

In Chapter 1, 'Color Marketing That Attracts People' (By Kim Byoung Hee), the process of color marketing activities in Shinan county, which pays special attention to colors that symbolize the socio-cultural background of the region, was thoroughly reviewed. This chapter introduces the concept and examples of color marketing, the color marketing activities of Purple island, and the domestic and international reactions to the color marketing of Purple island. At the same time, it also proposed strategic directions needed for developing color marketing activities suitable for each island's characteristics beyond the purple color of Purple island. Furthermore, it recommended carrying out color marketing activities to make Purple island an island with three values: an island of healing, an island of restoration, and an island of preservation.

Chapter 2, 'Green Marketing that Regenerates Regions with Flowers and Trees' (By Kim Byoung Hee and Hong Kyung Soo), highlights the value of the 'Flopia (Flower + Utopia)' project, which started in Shinan county in 2006, from various angles, in a situation where ESG management activities are becoming increasingly important in the public sector. In this chapter, the concept of green marketing, the structure and area of green marketing, green marketing using flowers and trees and green consumers, the Flopia project in Shinan county, and the expansion of Flopia and the future development direction were explored. Special attention was given to the fact that Shinan county's flower island project served as the basis for art islands and color islands and the foundation for green marketing.

Chapter 3, 'Art Marketing that Revives a Region through Art' (By Hong Kyung Soo), examines the value of art marketing that attempts to revitalize the region with artworks in Shinan county, the heaven of islands. In this chapter, the world of architectural art that can be encountered in the Floating Art Museum entering Anjwado island, the Infinito Art Museum entering Jaeundo island, the Sea Art Museum of Bigeumdo island and Anthony Gormley, and the Pilgrimage Path of the Gijeom-Soakdo island, and the "One Museum Per One Island Project" continuously promoted in Shinan county were introduced in detail. It also emphasized the fact that doubts about whether the establishment of a museum really helps Shinan county's regional regeneration were completely resolved by the participation of world-renowned artists.

In Chapter 4, 'For the Place Marketing Strategy of Shinan County' (By Kim Byoung Hee), it was explained that if place marketing activities are carried out, it establishes the identity of the region, improves the 'quality of life' of local residents, and also helps attract tourists. In this chapter, the concept and characteristics of place marketing, examples of place marketing, and a comprehensive analysis of Shinan county's place marketing strategy were carried out. And it proposed that six place marketing strategies: the deployment of integrated marketing communication, the establishment of tourism branding of Purple island, the exploration of diverse functions of museums and museums, the operation of village autonomy activities in Shinan county, the development of global marketing programs, and the deployment of mutually beneficial patronage activities, are the issues needed in Shinan county.

I would like to express my gratitude to Mr. Park Woo-ryang, the Mayor of Shinan County, for encouraging us to publish this book. I appreciate not only the deep interest he showed in this book but also the tremendous effort he has made to achieve many results for Shinan county. I also greatly appreciate the cooperation of Mr. Lee Jeong-su, Director of the Planning and Public Relations Office, and Mr. Joo Chun-kyu, Officer in Charge. I would like to express my gratitude to Mr. Kim Ji-man from the planning team for his assistance in proofreading. I extend my thanks to Mr. Kim Jin-hwan, CEO of Hakjisa, and Mr. Choi Im-bae, Vice President, who willingly published the book despite difficult publishing conditions, and to Mr. Kim Soon-ho, Director of the Editorial Department, and Ms. Kim Jin-young, Deputy Director, who reviewed the manuscript and made it a better book. Among the authors who wrote the manuscript with joy despite being busy, I would like to share the joy of publishing. From the planning to the deadline of the manuscript, it was never enough time, but the authors tried to write the manuscript by selecting only the necessary knowledge.

I hope that Korean public officials abroad, foreigners working in foreign public institutions, and foreign tourists planning to visit Korea will read this book. Also, I expect this book to serve as a guide, like a navigation system, to introduce the story of regional regeneration in Shinan county and Purple island both domestically and internationally. If you just take a quick look at the travel reviews that people who have visited Shinan county's Purple island have posted on Instagram or Meta (Facebook), it's undoubtedly 'Instagram+able.' Instagramable means 'worthy of being posted on Instagram,' a new term created by young people by combining Instagram, a photo-sharing social media, and the English word 'able.' Young people tend to choose their travel destinations depending on whether there are places to take pictures worthy of being posted on Instagram.

Many people who left travel reviews said they felt so happy just looking at the Purple Bridge spread out to the sea at the entrance of Purple island that they thought their trip was over. As the appearance of a 'purple cow' in the pasture, instead of yellow or white cows, would catch the eye, Purple island can certainly be considered a noteworthy travel destination like a purple cow. If you are a homo viator planning to visit Korea now, I would recommend you to visit the many islands of Shinan county in Jeollanam-do and set off into unfamiliar time. Go to the purple island! As the purple cow comes, the purple island will come. The purple, Purple island will be greeting you from afar. Let's go, Homo Viator!

March 2024

Kim Byoung Hee

Table of Contents

Here Comes The Purple Island

Chapter 1
Color Marketing that Attracts People

Kim Byoung Hee(Professor, Seowon University)

How can color draw people in? Among various factors constituting a landscape, color has a decisive influence on its composition. Color implies the social, economic, and cultural background of a region, and it also symbolizes its regional characteristics and lifestyle. Shinan county and its residents, considering the purple characteristics of the bellflower colony native to Banwoldo island and Bakjido island, created a purple island and started calling it 'Purple island.' Then, many people flocked to it, and it began to gain attention in the domestic and international media. The purple color had seduced people's hearts.

This kind of marketing activity that uses color to promote a subject is called color marketing. Marketing expert Seth Godin wrote a book called "Purple Cow" inspired by the idea that a purple cow appearing in a pasture, rather than a yellow or white cow, would capture people's attention. People were deeply attracted to the charm of Purple island when they saw the scenery filled with purple, from the Purple Bridge dyed in purple to the lavender garden of Bakjido island. In this chapter, we will take a look at the color marketing activities carried out in Shinan county.

1. The Concept and Cases of Color Marketing

Color marketing is a marketing technique that stimulates purchasing desires with a certain color. It is a marketing activity aimed at building brand assets using colors that people are likely to appreciate. Since color affects people's emotions and sentiments, the perspective that color is an important factor influencing decision-making underpins the basic logic of color marketing. In the 1920s, the fountain pens sold in the United States were black, but Parker discovered that red captured women's hearts and launched a red fountain pen. This is known as the beginning of color marketing. For example, a tourist at the entrance of Purple island in Shinan county, Jeollanam-do, may feel their heart fluttering and a rush of happiness just by looking at the 1,462m purple bridge (Purple Bridge) stretched out over the sea. This is the power of purple color marketing.[1]

It is known that visual stimuli influence consumers' purchasing decisions 87% of the time, followed by auditory 7%, tactile 3%, olfactory 2%, and gustatory 1%. Color marketing utilizes color to stimulate consumers' emotions, and it is a promising marketing technique in the digital media age where emotion has become important. In a situation where information is overflowing, injecting a certain color to consumers makes it easier to promote the brand. Color marketing, which was mainly used in the distribution industry, is now being emphasized in the public sector beyond corporations. The 'Color of the Year' announced annually by Pantone, a global color brand, has a significant impact on determining the direction of color marketing.

Let's take a look at brands that have actively carried out color marketing activities to build their brand assets. First, red reminds us of Coca-Cola. Red raises attention and also induces a sense of hunger, stimulating appetite. In 2011, Coca-Cola sold white cans as part of an environmentally friendly marketing activity to solve the polar bear problem, but due to consumers' protests, they switched back to red cans in just a month. Second, green signifies peace and stability. Starbucks has used green from its brand logo to its interior design. Naver also used green to create a peaceful and stable image. Third, blue symbolizes coldness and depression, but it also has a future-oriented feel, so it's preferred by information and communication companies. Samsung Electronics used blue to enhance the image of an innovative company. Fourth, black is dark but gives a sophisticated and modern feel. Fashion brands like Chanel emphasize luxury by contrasting black and white. Fifth, yellow gives a warm and friendly feel and is relatively noticeable. Kakao used yellow to create a friendly and bright corporate image. Sixth, purple has a mysterious and noble feel, so it is mainly used in high-end fashion brands. The luxury fashion brand Anna Sui built a distinctive brand image by emphasizing a high-quality image with purple.

The case of Market Kurly, which actively carried out color marketing activities using purple, also left implications for the color marketing activities of Shinan county's Purple island. Market Kurly, an online food delivery company, established its brand identity early on by deploying color marketing activities using purple. While dealing with organic ingredients, Market Kurly avoided the color green and also avoided red, which is known to stimulate appetite, instead choosing to use purple to imprint a luxurious image. Purple is a dye that can be obtained by collecting the secretion of a sea snail and drying it in the sun for several months, and it has been a symbol of wealth in both the East and West. Therefore, it attracted the interest of its main customer base, women, and consumers expressed satisfaction, considering that using Market Kurly was participating in environmentally friendly management. Furthermore, the dawn delivery at daybreak naturally resonated with housewives, earning their praise.[2]

Thus, color elements have a charm that moves people's hearts, which is why many companies have actively carried out color marketing activities using symbolic colors. The advantages of color marketing contribute to building brand assets, influence the formation of brand identity, are effective in attempting differentiation from competing brands, and stimulate the purchase desire for the brand.

[Figure 1-1] Brand sculpture of Purple island 'I PURPLE You'

Furthermore, if a specific color representing the brand is continually used to create a brand story, it can build a distinctive brand asset. Modern consumers dislike complexity and react easily to images, so color marketing activities focusing on a certain color are becoming increasingly important. The effectiveness of color marketing is also being proven in various studies.

For instance, in a study that clarified the impact of color marketing on brand image and revisit intentions in the restaurant industry, it was found that the associations and attention drawn by color marketing have a positive effect on brand image and customer satisfaction, and that the brand image has a positive effect on customer satisfaction and revisit intentions. This study provided a strategic direction to enhance customer satisfaction and loyalty by reemphasizing the importance of color marketing in the restaurant industry.[3]

In a study analyzing the relationship between color marketing and marketing performance, it was reported that the symbolism and associations created by color marketing influenced brand charisma. The symbolism of color had a significant effect on brand loyalty and brand satisfaction, the associations of color had an effect on brand loyalty, and the identifiability of color had an effect on brand satisfaction. This result implies that color marketing can be used as a means of customer attraction strategy and customer relationship management.[4]

Furthermore, in a study that conducted big data analysis on the landscape characteristics of Shinan county's Banwoldo island and Bakjido island, it was reported that landscape creation using colors influenced regional revitalization. The significance of the study lies in the fact that it found that the colors used in artificial facilities in Banwoldo island and Bakjido island, the first islands created with the theme of purple, formed a certain harmony with the surrounding environment, with a color series similar to the surrounding environment, and contrasting brightness and saturation values.[5)]

In a situation where tourists write about their favorite subjects in the photos they take at their destination, Purple island emerged as an attractive place to take photos. World-renowned photographers like Bae Byoung-woo and Michael Kenna have been capturing the scenery of Shinan county over several years. While taking photos, they are capturing various islands in Shinan county, including Purple island, from diverse angles. The district-specific colors determined through consultation between Shinan county and its residents in the color marketing project targeting 34 villages in 12 districts of Shinan county are purple, cobalt blue, bright yellow, crimson, and sky blue, and the color differentiation strategy will serve as a fundamental asset for revitalizing the tourism industry in Shinan county.

2. Color Marketing Activities of Shinan County's Purple Island

Shinan county is a paradise of islands, consisting of a total of 1,025 islands including 74 inhabited islands.[6] Each island has its unique cultural heritage and excellent natural landscapes. Jeollanam-do has been carrying out a project to preserve and regenerate the ecological resources and discover the culture of a total of 24 islands by adding two islands each year after implementing the 'Cultivating the Desired island Project' on six islands in Nando in 2015, up to 2024. Purple island refers collectively to Banwoldo island and Bakjido island, as shown in [Figure 1-2].

Banwoldo island, whose village topography is shaped like a half moon, is located at longitude 126°6′ and latitude 34°42′, with a total area of 1.97km^2, a coastline length of 6.7km, an average annual temperature of 14.1℃, and precipitation of 1,172mm. As of 2023, the population is 109 (52 males, 57 females) in 59 households. It is located 32km west of Mokpo Harbor.

Bakjido island, whose village topography is shaped like a

pot, is located at longitude 126°07′ and latitude 34°42′, with a total area of $1.19km^2$, a coastline length of 4.6km, an average annual temperature of 14.1℃, and precipitation of 1,172mm. As of 2022, the population is 34 (19 males, 15 females) in 24 households.[7]

Banwoldo island and Bakjido island, which gained the nickname Purple island, have been inhabited by humans since 1,000 years ago. In the 1980s, the population living on the two islands reached 700, but due to the effects of urbanization and industrialization, it has decreased to 143 in 2023. The residents of the two islands make a living from

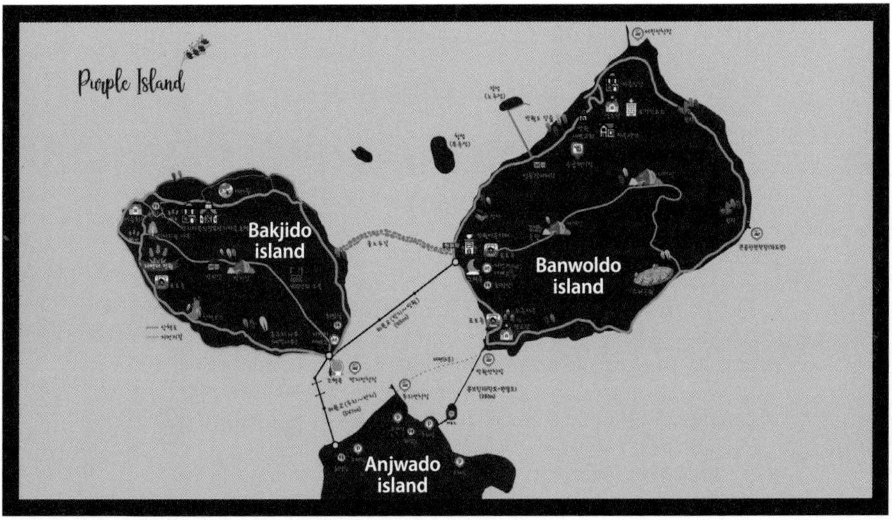

[Figure 1-2] The area encompassing Banwoldo island and Bakjido island, known as Purple island

nearshore fishing and activities in the mudflats while doing a little bit of farming. UNESCO has designated the entire island and the surrounding areas as the Shinan Dadohae Biosphere Reserve, and the government has also designated it as the Dadohae Marine National Park and the Mudflats Provincial Park, preserving the natural environment.

The attempt to revive the island, which was rapidly aging after the young people left, by activating its tourism resources, started from the proposal of the residents. The improvement of the landscapes and living environment of Banwoldo island and Bakjido island began when they were selected for the 'Cultivating the Desired island Project' in 2015. In the process of surveying the island's resources, it was confirmed that the residents of Banwoldo island were cultivating a lot of balloon flowers (also known as Platycodon grandiflorus), which bloom purple flowers, and there were many aster flowers on the island, which also bloom purple flowers. The colors of the balloon flowers, kohlrabi, and the aster flowers scattered all over the ground were all purple. Shinan county decided to carry out color marketing activities using purple, reflecting the ecological characteristics of Banwoldo island and Bakjido island. From 2015, public-private cooperation to cultivate Banwoldo island and Bakjido island as 'Purple Sanctuaries' began in earnest. Shinan county started the roof coloring work for landscape improvement of Banwoldo island and Bakjido island in early 2019. As a result, the roofs of 90 places in Banwoldo island, 30 places in Bakjido island, and 67 places in Duri village were colored purple. Looking at the roofs of the houses where the residents live, it's a world of purple.

The most noteworthy Purple Bridge on Purple island is a purple bridge totaling 1,462m, combining the 547m section between Duri village and Bakjido island and the 915m section between Bakjido island and Banwoldo island. The residents participated in all processes leading to the creation of a purple island, including the Purple Bridge, a purple bridge. The Purple Bridge, which started as a wooden bridge in 2007 as a new vitality project to hold the simple wish of Bakjido island resident Mrs. Kim Mae-geum who wanted to "walk out to the mainland with two feet", was completed in 2008. It was called 'Angel's Bridge' immediately after its completion.

However, when the elected county governor changed in July 2014, the 'Angel's Bridge' was renamed 'Bridge of

[Figure 1-3] Purple view of the Purple Bridge

[Figure 1-4] Purple night view of the Purple Bridge

Hope' in 2015, and was restored to 'Angel's Bridge' when county governor Park Woo-ryang took office again in July 2018. Although it was restored to 'Angel's Bridge', it faced the problem of renaming again as the bridge connecting Aphaedo island and Amtaedo island was approaching completion. During construction, it was called 'New Millennium Bridge', but since it was a name built around the time of the project's launch in 1998, it was confirmed as 'Cheonsa(1004) Bridge'[8] in late 2018, overlapping with the name 'Angel's Bridge'. 'Angel's Bridge' aged over time. The bridge was also named 'Purple Bridge'. The current Purple Bridge was born by coloring the Bridge of Hope in purple, inspired by the purple flowers of balloon flowers, kohlrabi, and aster. Near the Purple Bridge, they planted 120,000 lavender plants, 240,000 asta chrysanthemums, and 100,000 anemones that bloom purple flowers, creating a purple world.

Previously, you had to take a boat from the pier at Mokpo city's north harbor to get to the island, but it became much easier to access Purple island when the Angel Bridge opened in 2019. With the opening of Angel Bridge, everything from the bridge, coastal roads, roofs of houses

[Figure 1-5] Purple roof coloring of Bakji village in Bakjido island

[Figure 1-6] Purple lavender colony in Bakjido island

in the village, cars, parasols on the roadside, walls of small warehouses or buildings, residents' clothes, aprons, dishes, and coffee cups were all decorated in a uniform purple color. Residents planted asta chrysanthemums and magnolias and created lavender gardens. The lavender colonies cultivated by the residents create a spectacle in purple. The purple public phone in the lavender garden on Wind's Hill is also impressive. Shinan county and residents dyed the entire island in purple, from streetlights to payphones. The coastal promenade is a world of purple flowers including lavender, magnolias, hydrangeas, and purple radishes, so Purple island also gained a reputation as a 'purple heaven'.

In front of a café in Banwoldo island, the Little Prince and the desert fox from Antoine de Saint-Exupéry's novel "The Little Prince" (1943) are sitting on a purple half-moon sculpture, and there is also a purple tiger sculpture in front of the ticket office on Bakjido island. The sculpture of "The Little Prince" introduces a passage from the novel as follows: "It is the time you have wasted for your rose that makes your rose so important." Tourists take pictures in front of the sculpture of "The Little Prince", returning to the world of childhood. The subtle purple light emanating from the Purple Bridge creates a mysterious beauty when it meets the seawater at night.

In this way, a purple sanctuary that the world can admire was created on the small islands of Banwoldo island and Bakjido island. After the implementation of the 'Island Cultivation Project', the number of visitors has increased about twice, and when there are many tourists on the Purple Bridge, which cannot be crossed by car, there are often more than 1,000 people. As the Purple island, full of purple all year round, was born, people tired from their busy daily lives received comfort and emotion while looking at the beautiful scenery of Banwoldo island and Bakjido island. It can be evaluated that the purple color marketing transformed the rapidly aging island into a vibrant island.

Purple island, which has deployed color marketing for the entire island, is now attracting attention beyond national tourist spots. The Ministry of Culture, Sports and Tourism of the Republic of Korea has selected Purple island, a purple heaven all year round, as one of the 100 representative tourist destinations that you must visit. The

[Figure 1-7] Purple coloring of the Purple Bridge

[Figure 1-8] Purple coloring of a minivan on Purple island

Ministry of the Interior and Safety also selected Purple island as a good place to walk. You can walk 7.6 km to Banwoldo island, Purple Bridge, and Bakjido island through the 'Moon Bridge', and you can walk another 4.4 km along the coastal promenade to Bakjido island mountain. There is a bicycle rental shop at the entrance of Purple island, so it would be great to ride a bicycle and explore every corner of Purple island. Now, Purple island has truly earned a reputation as the best trekking course in the southwestern region.

Purple, combining the elegance of blue and the intensity of red, is depicted as a noble and attractive color preferred by kings in the Bible. Purple, which exists somewhere between blue and red, changes into various colors depending on the mixing ratio of blue and red. Associated with intuition, insight, imagination, pride, and tolerance, purple is a mysterious color symbolizing elegant and dignified splendor. People who like purple are said to be sensitive and have an excellent aesthetic sense, but on the other hand, they also reveal complex inner psychology such as emotional instability and jealousy or depression. When you want to express femininity, using purple is effective, as light purple gives an elegant and refined feeling. Purple is definitely a suitable color for attempting differentiation, but if used incorrectly, it can look vulgar or give an artificial feeling.

Nevertheless, it is important to note that purple is a color symbolizing healing. Tamiyo Suenaga, a Japanese color psychologist and color therapy expert, described the psychology of purple as 'the color that turns pain into healing power' in "Color Psychology" (2001). Human vitality has a tendency to maintain balance, and purple, a mix of red and blue, is said to give the impression of resolving conflicts. Tamiyo Suenaga noted the healing value of purple, saying, "In crisis situations, people are captivated by purple. Purple has the nature of trying to recover the balance of vitality in the process of turning into red, which gets vitality from gloomy blue." It means that people facing crisis fall into the charm of purple to heal their own conflicts. In other words, purple can be said to be a color of harmony and healing that cares for the heart.[9]

Seth Godin, a famous marketing expert, argued in "Purple Cow" (2003) that to move people's hearts, something must be more than just very good - it must be 'remarkable'. One day while traveling in rural France, the author found the scenery of cows peacefully grazing outside his car window pleasing, but as the scene continued, he began to feel bored. At that moment, he was inspired by the idea that if a purple cow appeared, not a yellow or white one, it would capture people's attention, leading him to write the book. The author defined 'remarkable' as something worth talking about. According to him, the opposite of 'remarkable' is not 'bad' or 'mediocre', but 'very good'. Just like the purple cow in his book, Purple island is a remarkable and charming space that captures attention.[10]

3. Domestic and International Reactions to the Color Marketing of Purple Island

The color marketing efforts of Shinan county were met with positive responses, and both domestic and foreign media had hot reactions to Purple island. After being introduced in Germany's Prosieben satellite broadcast and Hong Kong's popular travel magazine "U Magazine" in

2020, Purple island began to attract global attention.

"U Magazine" introduced Purple island as a 'hot spot' in Korea and extensively guided readers through its 6.2km purple road, Purple Bridge, and lavender gardens (U Magazine, 2020. 8. 28).[11] Global media outlet CNN referred to it as 'a dream island for photographers', presenting eight photos capturing various parts of the island (CNN, Feburary 8, 2021).[12]

Fox News also described it as a purple heaven perfect for Instagram pictures, detailing the transformation process of Banwoldo island into Purple island (Fox News, Feburary 19, 2021). ABS-CBN News, a television channel in the Philippines, forecasted a bright future for Purple island, reflecting its ecological environment (ABS-CBN News, March 16, 2021). WION, an Indian news channel, showcased the charms of Purple island, and was curious about how the purple symbol of BTS was related to Purple island (WION, March 15, 2021). Al Jazeera, the largest satellite broadcasting company in the Arab world, evaluated the transformation of Banwoldo island and Bakjido island as 'reinvention of the island' (Al Jazeera, May 25, 2021). Korean media also reported on the tourism value of Purple island while introducing foreign media (Yonhap News, Feburary 23, 2021).[13]

[Figure 1-9] CNN, USA (Feburary 8, 2021)

[Figure 1-10] Fox News, USA (Feburary 19, 2021)

[Figure 1-11] ABS-CBN News, Philippines (March 16, 2021)

[Figure 1-12] WION, India (March 15, 2021)

[Figure 1-13] Al Jazeera, Arab (May 25, 2021)

[Figure 1-14] Yonhap News, Korea (Feburary 23, 2021)

[Figure 1-15] U Magazine, Hong Kong (August 28, 2020)

[Figure 1-16] UN Best Tourism Villages Certificate (2021)

On December 2, 2021, at the United Nations World Tourism Organization (UNWTO) General Assembly held in Madrid, Spain, Purple island was selected as the '1st UN Best Tourism Village'. Established as a UN specialized agency in 1975, the UNWTO is responsible for coordinating tourism promotion policies, and is composed of 155 member countries including South Korea, six associate member countries, and over 400 branches. The UNWTO's Best Tourism Villages initiative evaluates and selects based on natural scenery including local food, cultural diversity, and efforts to protect rural community values. In competition with 170 villages from 75 countries around the world, Purple island was selected in the highest rank of the three levels. It was a very meaningful event in that the United Nations and the world recognized Shinan county's efforts to create islands with unique colors by preserving the ecological

[Figure 1-17] Promotional Material for Selection as 'World's Best Tourism Village' (2021)

environment and cultural characteristics of each island.

Shinan county produced promotional materials like [Figure 1-17] to announce that Purple island had been selected as the world's best tourism village by the UN, thereby greatly highlighting expectations for tourism activation. It is certain that Purple island will emerge as a new tourist attraction in Asia.[14] The source of Banwoldo island and Bakjido island being selected as 'World's Best Tourism Village' by the UN and winning the 'Star of Korean Tourism' was the energy from all the residents of Shinan county who agreed and cooperated that each island must show off its unique color charm to be competitive.

Interestingly, purple is the symbolic color of the world-renowned K-pop group BTS. It would be a fantastic combination if they regrouped to perform or shoot a music video on Purple island. In February 2022, an introductory video promoting Korean fashion was filmed on Purple island for a Paris fashion show. The video used the Purple Bridge as a runway stage against the backdrop of the sea and the island. Given that a small island in the southern province has even become known to the Paris fashion show, interest in Purple island will continue to explode.

4. Ongoing Color Marketing of Shinan County

In addition to the color marketing activities of Purple island, Shinan county has been conducting color marketing activities tailored to the characteristics of several islands. A representative example of this is the 'Cultivating the Desired island Project', which focused on improving the landscape. The process began by painting the roofs and gradually extended to painting colors on the entire island's sculptures. The touch of color marketing has been extended to the roofs of several island villages, from Banwoldo island and Bakjido island to Jaeundo island. The regional color projects that reflect the natural scenery of the island villages and the characteristics of each village have been carried out targeting 34 villages in 12 districts. The color marketing project, which has invested approximately 4.595 billion won in 2,520 places, will continue in the future.

The main colors for each district, decided through consultation between Shinan county and its residents, were purple, cobalt blue, bright yellow, and crimson. The reason Shinan county actively carried out color marketing activities was to attract tourists, secure tourism resources, and express individuality for each district suitable for the characteristics of each island. In this process, the living environment naturally improved as well. Specific examples of roof coloring can be seen from [Figure 1-18] to [Figure 1-22].

The examples of color marketing carried out in each district are interesting. For example, the roofs of Seondo island Village in Jido-eup were painted bright yellow. Seondo island of Jido-eup is home to about 270 people in about 160 households. The island gained the nickname 'island of Narcissuss' after old women Hyun Bok-soon, who moved to Seondo island after retirement, started growing about ten kinds of Narcissuss in her front yard over ten years ago. In March 2019, they held an island Narcissus festival by planting 27 main species and over 100 world species on an area of 12.3 ha, the largest scale in the country. Based on this history, Seondo island Village completed roof coloring in bright yellow, the color of Narcissuss, in December 2020. And in several villages on

[Figure 1-18] Island of Pilgrims, Soakdo island, Crimson roof coloring of Dae-Gijeom island (Bigger particle island of Gijeom) village

[Figure 1-19] Island of Pilgrims, Soakdo island, Crimson roof coloring of So-Gijeom island (Smaller particle island of Gijeom) village

[Figure 1-20] Uido island (also known as Baek Seohyang's island), Cobalt blue roof coloring of Jin-ri village

[Figure 1-21] Uido island (also known as Baek Seohyang's island), Red roof coloring of Donmok village

[Figure 1-22] Seondo island (also known as Narcissus island), Bright yellow roof coloring of Seondo village in Seondo island

[Figure 1-23] 'Purple Sikhye' and 'Yellow Sikhye' from Shinan County Agricultural Product Processing Center

Uido island, the roofs were painted cobalt blue, the sea color often used in the paintings of artist Kim Whan-ki.

Furthermore, Shinan county has expanded its color marketing activities to the 'agricultural product processing field' and is continuously releasing products like 'color sikhye' (a sweet rice beverage). In July 2022, the Shinan County Agricultural Product Processing Center released 'Purple Sikhye' and 'Yellow Sikhye' made from high-quality rice produced in Shinan. The color sikhye launched by the Shinan County Agricultural Product Processing Center comes in two types: 'Purple Sikhye' made using purple sweet potatoes and 'Yellow Sikhye' with sweet pumpkins. Both types of color sikhye have completed HACCP certification and their own quality inspections.

Purple Sikhye is a traditional beverage that retains its traditional taste while symbolizing the purple color of Purple island. Yellow Sikhye applies the color of blooming Narcissuss to sweet pumpkins, much like the bright yellow roof color of Seondo island Village in Jido-eup. The Shinan County Agricultural Product Processing Center plans to first supply these sikhye to representative tourist spots of Shinan, such as Purple island, Byeongpungdo island, and

Odo island, and gradually distribute them through online shopping malls and general stores. As the nature of incubating small-scale processing businesses is strong, anyone in Shinan county who is interested in color marketing activities can try it.

5. Significance of Purple Island's Color Marketing

An ordinary island, which was not even known as a tourist spot, was dyed purple and rose to prominence as a popular destination attracting a lot of attention both domestically and internationally. More and more visitors have spread the word that Purple island is a great place for photo shoots. The transformation of an ordinary island into a famous tourist destination, such as Purple island, was significantly influenced by the color marketing planning skills of the Shinan county office and the active participation of the island residents. Therefore, Purple island can be considered a representative example of successful place marketing focused on color.

In color marketing, color is utilized as the core message to carry out marketing activities. As the functionality and quality of tourist products have become similar, people are becoming more interested in the unique sentiments of tourist products. Because color marketing sells the sentiment of a certain region, the visual image that forms the impression is important. Although many local governments have emphasized the importance of color marketing so far, it seems that almost only Purple island has properly executed it by connecting it with place marketing. To become a notable place, it must have visitability, livability, and investability. Among these, visitability is the most important, and Purple island has already secured it.

Moving forward, Shinan county and the residents should more systematically carry out color marketing activities for Purple island. In color marketing activities for Purple island, a strategy should be established to increase the visitability, which makes people want to visit, by harmonizing the ecological characteristics of Banwoldo island and Bakjido island with the surrounding environment. As Purple island chose the color purple to differentiate itself from other areas, it should carry out color marketing activities that more clearly highlight the brightness and saturation, considering landscape elements such as the island, sea, sky, purple bridge, and purple roofs.

The future vision of Purple island lies in revitalizing the island through tourism. However important tourism development might be, it should not precede the issue of ecosystem protection. Residents and visitors should share this understanding and strive to cultivate and preserve the ecological environment. Good examples include designating a closed fishing season (every year from June 21 to July 20) to maintain the main source of income, octopus fishing, and setting up an 'Octopus Kindergarten' to protect young octopuses. Even if it is somewhat inconvenient for tourists, programs necessary for carbon zero tourism and green tourism should also be introduced. Furthermore, Purple island has community culture, like local festivals that reflect the unique characteristics of the island, and efforts should be made to strengthen and restore traditional culture.

Moreover, the beautiful living culture of Purple island, which aims to revive the 'neighborhood culture' of happily getting along with neighbors, should also be established. When operating a tourism program with public funding, it should not be entrusted to individual island residents or outsiders, but should be entrusted to an organization in which island residents participate collectively. For this, Shinan county enacted an ordinance related to the operation of Purple island in 2020, and established a systematic mechanism to distribute tourism income appropriately to marginalized groups who do not directly engage in the tourism industry.

The success of the best tourism villages depends on the support and participation of the residents. Shinan county must jointly find tourism-related issues with the residents of each village and prepare ways for residents to participate. For example, residents need job creation such as cooking in a village restaurant, working as a barista in a village cafe, driving an electric car around the village, and creating purple gardens everywhere. Shinan county also needs to search for realistically useful policies, strategies, and action plans to preserve Shinan's cultural and natural assets and activate the three elements of tourism (economy, society, environment). If the following four aspects are considered in future color marketing activities in Shinan county, it will show more than expected results.[15]

First, the preservation of cultural and natural assets is important. The preservation of cultural assets should be approached from the perspective of restoring forgotten cultures. The village's traditional festivals disappeared as the residents aged, but new young populations influx can restore traditional culture. The unique ritual of Purple island that strengthens community bonds by wishing for a good blowfish catch should also be restored, and reckless development should be avoided to preserve natural assets. Measures such as recommending bicycle tourism or walking tourism to tourists should also be considered. Restrictions should be placed on the use of tidal flats only when necessary for a minimum livelihood to protect them, and activities to set a closed fishing season or protect young fish should also be developed.

Second, the economic aspect is also important. If tertiary (or service) industries like tourism are not introduced to Purple island, which has a high dependency on primary industries, residents may become economically impoverished or face the crisis of regional extinction. Therefore, the pristine ecological resources on Purple island should be utilized and tourism activation projects led by local residents should be promoted to create high added value in the long term. Local residents should benefit economically by engaging in various tourism industries, and the income from entrance fees and other common income should be fairly redistributed to improve the quality of life of all residents.

Third, the social aspect is also important. An alternative that can overcome phenomena such as local extinction or population cliff that Purple island is currently facing should be urgently prepared. For example, by actively accommodating the returning farming and returning population migrating from other regions to Shinan county, issues such as local extinction or population cliff can be solved. A stepping stone should also be prepared for young people who left Shinan county to return to their hometown with the activation of the tourism industry. Moreover, policies that actively support people who are interested in the tourism-related industries of Shinan county and want to migrate to Shinan county should also be promoted. Through these processes, Purple island's social assets will also grow.

Fourth, the environmental aspect is also important. If

vitality is injected into Purple island in a state where the natural ecology and unique culture of Shinan county are appropriately combined, the value of Purple island will shine in the future. If the entire Purple island is designated as a tourist village and developed into a sustainable village, more domestic and foreign tourists will visit Purple island. This is why Shinan county needs to pay special attention to the issue of environmental protection on Purple island. In the future, it will be necessary to launch an environmental protection campaign to refrain from visiting the island by car. And systematic devices to prevent littering and protect the ecological environment should also be prepared.

If Purple island continues to maintain its symbolism of 'I Purple You,' it can fully achieve its future vision. V of BTS, a leading player in Hallyu content, said "I Purple You," which means "I love you." It contains the intention to love together until the end, like the last color of the seven-colored rainbow, purple. Based on the purple color asset, color marketing activities should be carried out to turn Purple island into an island with three values.

First, as an island of healing, it should be a place people want to visit. The Purple island of the past was an ordinary island village untouched by tourists. However, since the launch of color marketing activities, it has been reborn as an island that tourists visit to enjoy the natural scenery and the spectacle of purple. In the future, Shinan county should make Purple island an island of healing that visitors want to revisit by offering unique and diverse experiences.

Second, as an island of restoration, it should be a place people want to return to. Purple island is experiencing a rapid decrease in population and an increase in the elderly population. However, after launching tourism businesses and color marketing, a variety of jobs were created on Purple island. The number of natives who left for the city in search of jobs and then returned to their hometowns to start new jobs also increased. In order to bring back natives who left and attract creative young people from outside to Purple island for a new life, Shinan county should actively operate a 'return' program.

Third, as an island of preservation, it should be a resurrecting island. There are many neglected natural and cultural heritages on Purple island while the aging of residents is progressing. Examples include the pufferfish festival to wish for a good catch, a fire game to wish for a good year, and the story of the Jungnodu path that wishes for a thousand years of love. In the future, Shinan county should not spare policy support to restore the natural and cultural heritage of Purple island. Everyone should make an effort to resurrect island culture by preserving natural heritage and reproducing cultural heritage.

Interesting stories have remarkable values. If a purple cow walks into a pasture where there are yellow cows, spotted cows, and black cows, it can't help but stand out. If a purple cow appears in the meadow, not a yellow or white cow, it must really attract attention. Seth Godin imagined such a scene and wrote a book called "Purple Cow." If a swan is walking in a field where a flock of crows are squawking, its elegant figure will shine even more. The purple cow symbolizes creative thinking in color marketing.

The same goes for Purple island. So far, Shinan county has carried out color marketing activities that are outstanding anywhere. Many stories were also created among tourists. If a good story is created, the story itself is a product. People who have visited Purple island often post their travel reviews on Instagram or Facebook. Many say that they felt happy just by looking at the Purple Bridge spread out to the sea at the entrance of Purple island. So, it can definitely be said that Purple island is a remarkable travel destination, like a purple cow. When you go there, a purple island will come just like a purple cow does. Homo viator (traveling people), let's head to Purple island.

Here Comes The Purple Island

Chapter 2
Green Marketing that Regenerates Regions with Flowers and Trees

Kim Byoung Hee(Seowon University)
Hong Kyung Soo(Ajou University)

As we enter the digital age, green marketing activities are becoming increasingly important. The term 'green' implies 'eco-friendly' and 'non-artificial', but there are various discussions about what green actually means in reality. Green marketing aims to protect the Earth's environment and live a nature-friendly life. Flower festivals are always popular among people. How exactly do flowers attract people? The 'Flopia (Flower+Utopia)' project attempted by Shinan county is an effort to plant flowers unique to the island to attract people.

The Flopia project, which started in 2006, became the basis for the green marketing attempted by Shinan county. Flowers have their own inherent natural beauty. Therefore, any flower gives off a sense of sophisticated aesthetic beauty. Not only in its formative beauty, but flowers also have enchanting colors and unique fragrances, and their green stems and leaves offer a refreshing sense of nature. Especially when one type of flower fills a wide field, it even adds a sense of sublimity due to its large scale. In this chapter, we look at Shinan county's flower island project, the origin of the art island and color island, from the perspective of green marketing.

1. Concept of Green Marketing

In 1972, the World Environment Conference was held in Stockholm under the theme of 'Only One Earth'. The core content of the declaration announced at that time is as follows: "Humans have the right to freedom, equality, and a prosperous life in a pleasant environment where the dignity and welfare of life are allowed." Through such a process, the awareness that companies must fulfill their social responsibilities for environmental protection has spread. From the perspective of profit-seeking companies, they initially agreed in principle with environmental protection issues but judged that there were conflicting elements.

However, businesses are now in an era where survival is impossible if they exist solely for the pursuit of profit from a short-sighted perspective. Companies that do not fulfill their social responsibilities as members of the social community or ignore environmental problems can no longer expect growth. The sociocultural background in which green marketing emerged is a problem caused by environmental pollution as people have come to enjoy material abundance due to the acceleration of industrial society. The reason businesses started to pay attention to green marketing was due to the spread of environmental conservation consciousness among consumers.

Consumers interested in quality of life began to have a deep interest in environmental issues and started monitoring corporate activities. The global village is rapidly becoming desolate due to industrialization and urbanization. Within the company, there was a reflection on managerial marketing that ignores public interest and only pursues profit. As environmental centrism and consumer centrism were highlighted, companies also began to modify their existing marketing directions. The direction of corporate marketing activities also changed from a traditional consumer-oriented perspective to an environmentally friendly socio-ecological perspective.

Companies also began to emphasize sustainable

development. In the field of marketing, discussions on marketing and ecological crises have been held since the 1970s, showing a main interest in ecology and environmental and green marketing. Most studies have revealed the characteristics of consumers who show distinctive interest in environmental topics or behaviors such as resource recycling, pollution, and energy conservation. In many countries, including Europe, products that do not meet the demands of green consumers do not sell, so companies have strengthened their green marketing activities. If you are only interested in increasing profits, it's immoral and in a reality where corporate citizenship is highlighted, the social responsibility of companies has been further emphasized.

Green marketing refers to all corporate marketing activities related to environmental conservation, and is a marketing strategy that emphasizes corporate social responsibility and marketing activities respecting human beings aiming to improve the quality of life. In an environment where corporate social responsibility is important, companies must also accept various conditions suitable for environmental changes at a strategic level. While the traditional concept of marketing was limited to corporate activities providing products and services that can satisfy customers, since the concept of green marketing emerged, social responsibility in corporate activities has become more important than anything else.

Until the start of green marketing, the reason for a company's existence was to maximize profits with minimal costs from product development to pricing, distribution, and promotion. However, since the late 1980s, companies have started to consider consumers not as simple product buyers but as objects of consideration. In green marketing activities, there was also an awakening that it is necessary to sell products and services that meet consumer needs and aim for socio-ecological balance and human welfare. In other words, green marketing had a decisive impact on spreading 'consumer centrism'.

2. Structure and Scope of Green Marketing

What is the structure of green marketing? The concept of green marketing does not need to be perceived in a narrow field such as environmental conservation or recycling from the profit dimension of a company. Green marketing should be recognized as a broad concept aimed at improving the quality of human life in terms of marketing functions and goals. The orientation of green marketing is for companies to fulfill their social responsibilities to improve the quality of human life. Green marketing is naturally characterized by normative marketing that naturally needs to perform activities necessary for society, focusing on the interdependence of humans and society. Therefore, green marketing forms a structure where stakeholders such as consumers, companies, and governments come together, and each entity influences each other. The relationships between stakeholders are as follows.

First, the safety needs of consumers act as a motivation to participate in environmental movements. Consumers can boycott products of companies that disregard environmental protection and can influence government environmental policies. Second, it is difficult for companies to disregard consumer demands and sometimes feel pressure. Companies that do not consider environmental issues may become extinct in the competitive environment due to government regulations or consumer pressure. Third, the government can recommend and regulate companies and consumers for the welfare of the people. The government can encourage consumers to recycle consumer goods, and the government can force companies to follow government environmental policies through administrative regulations.

Green marketing is deeply related to environmental protection (E), one of the ESG management issues that have recently emerged as a topic in corporate management. ESG is a management philosophy that corporate sustainable growth is possible only when practicing non-financial elements such as environmental protection (Environment), social contribution (Social), and governance (Governance, ethical management or governance improvement). Therefore, companies are exploring ways to create sustainable value by establishing organizations, formulating strategies, and preparing execution plans to establish ESG philosophy.

In relation to the value orientation of corporate management, terms such as corporate social responsibility (CSR), creating shared value (CSV), and ESG have been used interchangeably among experts. Compared to corporate social responsibility or creating shared value, ESG, which emerged recently, is a perspective to seek financial safety by linking environmental protection, social contribution, and governance elements in corporate management and financial activities. As the key is whether to trust the sustainability of the company, it emphasizes non-financial indicators that can measure sustainability. Ultimately, the core of ESG can be said to be sustainable investment value and social value. Companies are making efforts to strengthen ESG activities and show the results of social practice tasks.

The policy areas related to environmental protection (E) in the ESG evaluation items used in Bloomberg's corporate evaluation include energy efficiency, eco-friendliness, sustainable material use, climate change response, biodiversity, and eco-friendly product development.

Furthermore, the concept of sustainable development was also proposed as a reflection that human development could reach its limits due to environmental destruction was discussed centered around international organizations. The World Commission on Environment and Development (WCED) formally defined the concept of sustainable development in the report "Our Common Future" announced in 1987. In that report, it was defined as "development that meets the needs of the present generation without compromising the ability to meet the needs of future generations". Recently, its meaning has been expanded to development considering economic development, social integration, and environmental sustainability.

In September 2015, the UN General Assembly adopted the resolution 'Transforming Our World: The 2030 Agenda for Sustainable Development.' This document contains 17 goals and 169 detailed objectives that the world agreed to collectively achieve by 2030 for the sustainable development of humanity. Here, the Sustainable Development Goals (SDGs) refer to the 17 policy goals that the world has agreed to achieve together by 2030 for the sustainable development of humanity, which were agreed upon at the UN General Assembly in September 2015. The core of the goal achievement is inclusivity, embodied in the phrase "Leaving no one behind."

Because problems such as poverty, inequality, climate crisis, and violence, faced by all earthlings, cannot be resolved by the efforts of a specific group or country alone and require a joint response to related issues, the SDGs become inevitably important. In March 2017, the UN developed 232 indicators, which were adopted at the UN General Assembly in July of the same year. In 2020, 36 indicators were revised, and as of 2023, they are operating on a system of 231 indicators. The UN has assigned international organizations as the responsible parties for each indicator, assigned them the role of developing indicator methodologies and collecting data, and designated national SDGs data responsibility agencies for each country. In South Korea, the Statistical Development Institute of thc Statistics Agency has been designated as the 'UN SDGs Data National Responsibility Agency,' providing data related to 24 domestic indicators in cooperation with related ministries.

The mass consumption of modern society, based on materialism, has caused environmental problems and, as a result, has lowered the quality of life and highlighted the issue of human survival. If the concept of green marketing is recognized not as a narrow concept such as environmental preservation or recycling in the dimension of corporate profit-seeking, but as a broad concept for enhancing the 'quality of life' of humans.[1] The field of green marketing includes the basic structure of the environment, living conditions, and all areas of human life in a social and cultural context. Green marketing should be distinguished from the traditional concept of marketing in that it emphasizes corporate social responsibility.

3. Utilization of Flowers and Trees in Green Marketing and Green Consumers

Green advertising is the act of expressing green marketing as a concrete message to prompt people's actions. Green advertisements can be differentiated by taking human attitudes towards nature as the horizontal axis (anthropocentrism vs. ecocentrism) and political perspectives as the vertical axis (reformism vs. radicalism). There are differences in the objectives of green advertising depending on these classifications.[2] Kilbourne argues that there are five types of green advertisements, such as environmentalism, conservationism, human welfare ecology, preservationism, and ecologism, depending on the functional relationship between human attitudes towards nature and political perspectives.[3]

The green marketing of Shinan county is being carried out at various levels, ranging from environmentalism to ecologism. In relation to local government's ESG management, Shinan county is leading in carbon neutrality by creating a 10-kilometer-long tree-lined road and an ecological restoration forest. While the government is promoting the '2050 Carbon Neutrality Declaration' and 'Establishment of 2050 Scenarios' to minimize domestic damage due to climate change and actively respond to climate crises, Shinan county is making efforts to solve the carbon neutrality problem. As a recent measure to overcome the climate crisis, Shinan county has created fine dust barrier forests, a 10-kilometer-long tree-lined road, living zone forests, and ecological restoration forests to enhance the absorption capacity of forest carbon sinks. For example, look at the beauty of the 10-kilometer-long tree-lined road on Dochodo island in Shinan county, as shown in [Figure 2-1]. Shinan county identifies tree resources suitable for local climate and growing conditions nationwide and plants a large number of trees at the appropriate time using donated trees with landscape value. A Shinan county official stated, "We will strive to enhance the economic and ecological value of forests by creating unique forests in Shinan county, such as creating urban forests for carbon neutrality offset and expanding carbon sinks for marine ecosystem protection, and actively participating in responding to climate crises."[4]

[Figure 2-1] 10-ri(about 4km)-long tree-lined road in Dochodo island

Corporate green marketing and green advertising attempt for product production and sales to prevent environmental pollution, but in the case of local governments rather than corporations, many attempts are made to protect the local environment and regenerate the deteriorated environment using flowers and trees. For example, if you visit Hokkaido, Japan, you can enjoy various flowers. Every summer, many tourists flock to see the beautiful flower fields, especially lavender fields, on this island located in the northernmost part of Japan. In the Hokkaido region, you can see flower fields that cannot be found anywhere else in the world. The top 10 places to see flowers in Hokkaido include Farm Tomita, famous for its lavender flowers, Shibazakura Park located north of Mt. Mokoto where a million cherry blossoms bloom every spring, Kamiyubetsu Tulip Park, the most famous tulip spot in Hokkaido, Shikisai no Oka Garden where flowers bloom all year round according to the flowering season in a garden that reaches 15ha, and Hokuryu Sunflower Village where you can enjoy walking among two million sunflowers.[5)]

Shinan county has been promoting the creation of FLOPIA islands, where flowers bloom all year round

(FLOPIA, a portmanteau of 'flower' and 'utopia'). Shinan county plans to invest more than 10 billion won annually to turn several islands in the county into FLOPIA islands, starting with the Narcissus festival on Seondo island. Various flower and tree festivals are also held on many islands of Shinan county. These include the Narcissus Festival on Seondo island, the Canola Flower Festival on Jido island, the Red Camellia Garden Festival and the Shinan Tulip Festival on Imjado island, the Baby Camellia Festival on Aphaedo island.

On Jeungdo island, the country's first Slow City, aromatic trees such as Magnolia grandiflora Tree and Pittosporum tobira continue to be planted. Magnolia Kobus are planted on Jaeundo island, Mulberry Trees that reminisce about artist Kim Whan-ki on Anjwado island, and Lilac clusters on Banwoldo and Bakjido island. A Hallabong Tangerine garden on Hauido island, a garden of red flowers such as Korean Rosebay on Bigeumdo island, a Hydrangea garden on Dochodo island, a World Camellia Park on Aphaedo island, and a White garden with Silver Magnolia on Jangsando island, are all currently being created in Shinan county.

In relation to Shinan county's FLOPIA green marketing, the 'Bangsik Art Center Shinan Campus,' which broke ground on February 19, 2022, and started construction, is significant in that a flower decoration specialty education institution is entering Apaeup in Shinan county. The Bangsik Art Center Shinan Campus was completed in 2023 with a private capital injection of 4.3 billion won on a site of 24,193 square meters in Daecheon-ri, Apaeup. Director Bangsik, who has been expressing beauty with flowers and nature for over 50 years since 1972, is a renowned garden master recognized by Germany and the first Oriental

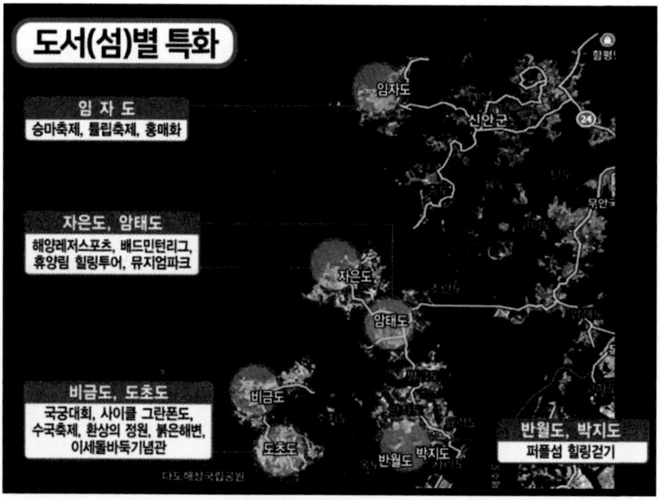

[Figure 2-2] The blueprint for Shinan county's regional specialized sports tourism industry

Meister Florist. Director Bang, who was also in charge of flower decorations for the opening and closing ceremonies of the 1988 Seoul Olympics, expressed his intention to turn the Bangsik Art Center Shinan Campus into a cradle of flower art experts in line with Shinan county's FLOPIA policy. The Bangsik Art Center Shinan Campus will include classrooms, workrooms, a botanical garden, and an administration building to train domestic and international flower decoration experts.

Moreover, Shinan county is developing a regional specialized industry linked to FLOPIA and sports events based on the support of the Korea Sports Promotion Foundation. The blueprint for Shinan county's regional specialized sports tourism industry is as shown in [Figure 2-2]. The project to foster a regional specialized sports tourism industry is a business that develops new sports tourism programs linked to local core tourism resources and leisure sports and seeks regional development. Shinan county has set the 'FLOPIA Sports Festival', which is linked to FLOPIA where flowers bloom all year round and the "One Museum Per One island Project" policy, as its main concept and introduced the Cycle Gran Fondo (a noncompetitive amateur competition) in Bigeumdo and Dochodo island, a badminton league in the central region, a marine leisure sports festival on Jaeundo island, a beach horse riding festival on Imjado island, and a Purple island healing walking program on Anjwado island.

Along with active discussions on green marketing, the terms green consumption and green consumers are often used. Green consumption refers to the consumer behavior of preferring products produced by environmentally friendly or environmentally proactive companies and having the willingness to purchase products that improve environmental outcomes. Green consumers, similar to environmentally friendly consumers, are those who actively prefer products with relatively less negative impact on the environment. Green consumers are likely to have a deeper interest in Shinan county's FLOPIA green marketing utilizing flowers and trees. This is because they set environmental protection as a criterion for consumption behavior and strive for a consumer life that considers environmental issues.

The behavioral characteristics of green consumers vary greatly depending on the personal preferences of consumers.

However, the universal traits of green consumers are that they require environmental information, strive for differentiation from general consumers, and desire the maintenance of existing lifestyles. The general purchasing process goes through five stages such as recognizing needs and desires, searching for related information, evaluating alternatives, making purchasing decisions, and post-purchase behavior. The purchase process of green consumers and general consumers has similar aspects, but the considerations at the purchasing stage are significantly different.

Korea is also now entering the growth stage of green marketing. Globally, as ESG management is emerging as an essential factor for corporate survival, the number of green consumers is increasing. Shinan county's efforts to lead in carbon neutrality by creating a 10-ri[6] path of poplar trees and restoring an ecological forest can be said to have changed the paradigm of policy from carbon-centered to green-centered. Shinan county's FLOPIA project is a successful case of practically implementing green marketing. Shinan county's attempts are a good example that it is important to practice in reality, not just proclaiming

ESG management in the public sector. Let's take a closer look at Shinan county's FLOPIA project, which has been unfolded from the perspective of green marketing.

4. The Flopia Project of Shinan County

1) The Miracle of Seondo island Brought by Narcissus

One of the most representative success stories of the Flopia Project is Seondo island, the island of Narcissus. Seondo island belongs to Jido-eup, located 51km northwest of Mokpo city. With a total area of 5.600km^2, as of 2021, it is a small island where 169 households, or 287 people, reside. The island is also known as Mapjae or Seonchido because its shape resembles a cicada.[7] Seondo island, with its irregular shipping routes and unfamiliar name, attracted over 12,000 tourists during the 10-day Narcissus Festival in 2019. This might be the record for the most visits since the island was formed. But how did Seondo island become the island of Narcissus?

(1) The First Step of Grandma, Hyun Bok-soon

I visited Seondo island in July 2022.[8] It was well after the peak of spring when the Narcissus is in full bloom, so I couldn't see the spectacle of Narcissus dyed yellow. However, the village looked very bright and vibrant with roofs painted yellow and walls painted white. The first place I visited was 'The House of Narcissus' near Judong Church. It was the house of old women Hyun Bok-soon,

[Figure 2-3] Seondo island, the island of Narcissus, started with old women Hyun Bok-soon's Narcissus

the first person to grow Narcissus on Seondo island. Currently, she's in a nursing home, and the house was empty. Yet, it seemed as if her touch still remained in the garden, perhaps due to her dedication.

Born and raised in Mokpo city, old women Hyun Bok-soon left her life on the mainland and moved to the island following her husband's desire to return to his hometown, Seondo island, about 30 years ago. Having spent her entire life on the mainland and with all her children having left home, she had no particular regrets. She loved flowers since she was young. Her family home in Mokpo had a spacious garden where clematis, honeysuckle, and Korean rosebay flowers bloomed seasonally. With the money from selling an apartment in Seoul, she built a small house in the middle of a 700-pyeong[9] (approximately 2,320 square meters) field on Seondo island, with a considerable space left over. From that point, she started to cultivate a garden in her home's yard. She first planted forsythia and clematis around the house as a fence. In early spring, forsythias bloomed, and when they faded, roses bloomed in full from May. Whenever she had to go to the mainland, she bought flowers to plant and cultivate. She also planted poppies and lilies. About 20 years ago, she bought two roots of Narcissus from a farm and planted them. Particularly fond of the color white, she is said to have planted many white Narcissus.[10]

The locals couldn't understand why she didn't farm but only cultivated flowers, but She devoted herself to planting and cultivating flowers. During a local election, county governor Park Woo-ryang visited Seondo island. Having seen the Narcissus, Mayor Park suggested turning Seondo island into an island of Narcissus. After being elected in the 2018 election, he immediately requested residents to plant Narcissus, but there were almost no participants. Therefore, in cooperation with the council, he established the "Ordinance on the Creation and Support of the Narcissus island of Shinan county." This ordinance promised to compensate residents as much as the harvest of garlic and onions if they planted Narcissus. Then he immediately prepared for the festival. He created the largest Narcissus field in the country, equivalent to the size of 16 football fields (12.3ha), by reclaiming the abandoned wasteland and farmland. At this site, 2 million roots of over 100 species of Narcissus from around the world were planted for the 2019

Narcissus Festival, which was a great success with 12,000 visitors.

Before becoming the island of Narcissus, Seondo island was reportedly a dark and quiet island. The roads were either non-existent or very narrow, making movement inconvenient. With no supermarkets or restaurants, it was a weakly prominent island. As the lights would all turn off in the evening, it was so dark and quiet that it was called a goblin island. The islanders naturally accepted their inconvenient lives, lagging in development, and lived from generation to generation. However, as Seondo island made its name known as the island of Narcissus, it became an island visited by over 10,000 tourists, with well-paved roads and elevated consciousness of the residents. It transformed from a dark and inconvenient island into a bright and clean village.

(2) Changes Brought by Flowers

Although I visited in the hot month of July and was not able to see the beautiful narcissus flowers in bloom, signs with the names of narcissus varieties written on them were noticeable all along the road from Sundew Port to Judong

Church. Feeling the strenuous efforts of the villagers who cultivated the village, I could imagine this expansive garden and hill filled with narcissus. The village seemed bright and beautiful, painted with the light yellow color of narcissus.

I met Park Ki-nam, the chairman of the festival committee overseeing the Narcissus Festival. Chairman Park returned to his hometown six years ago after living away. He wanted to live a relaxed life, catching octopus and doing woodworking, but he took on the responsibility of the festival committee because someone was needed to

[Figure 2-4] Seondo island, with the goal of creating an island filled with narcissus

prepare for the festival. His role is to lead the participation of villagers in planting and managing the narcissus. With the average age of the villagers in their mid-60s, it is difficult and important to organize people to water, manage, and weed in Seondo island, where there is a shortage of laborers. He persuaded landowners who used to plant beans, onions, and garlic to plant narcissus, and rented the land by ensuring the income they would get from growing onions and garlic instead of planting narcissus. In 2021, they even sold roots worth 60 million won to a botanical garden in Asan, but from 2022, they agreed to expand the cultivation area in Seondo island without exporting roots. Seondo island, which has the most varieties of narcissus cultivation and the largest cultivation area in Korea, will be filled with narcissus all over the island in the future.

Has there been a change in the villagers' thoughts since it changed to the island of Narcissus? Chairman Park said that there has been an enormous change, and that even if they were given flowers or roots in the past, they did not plant them, but after holding the festival once, they want to plant them and ask each other to do so. He said he realized,

"Flowers can change people like this. This is the power of flowers." Even during non-festival periods, he said he was happy that more than 100 people came in the spring of 2022, and that there were also people coming to see the chrysanthemums planted along with the narcissus. "The more people visit, the better. It's gratifying and good when people come to the island where people didn't come before. I am proud of myself and try to do my work even if I sometimes get scolded by the residents."

"It's so beautiful." There is overflowing pride in the

[Figure 2-5] The summit of the Hydrangea Park where Olafur Eliasson's 'Earth Cultural Facility' will be installed

[Figure 2-6] Bird's-eye view of Olafur Eliasson's Earth Cultural Facility

transformed village. Chairman Park, who is happy due to the request to include the village, not just the festival area, in the festival, said that the hometown association living away from home shows a lot of interest and visits more often. "Our Seondo island has become so good." He said that the hometown people take pride in their improved hometown.

2) The island of Hydrangeas and Camphor Trees, Dochodo island

(1) The Trendiest Flower, Hydrangea

The flower that is currently gaining popularity is the hydrangea. Even as someone unfamiliar with flowers, the flower I have seen the most recently is the hydrangea. The hydrangeas I saw in Jeju Boromwat and those covering Goheung Ssuk island were impressive for their abundant and elegant beauty. Hydrangea, originally from China, mainly grows in three countries: Korea, China, and Japan. The initial blossoming hydrangea is a white flower with a hint of green, which gradually changes to a bright blue, and finally changes to a purple with a hint of red. It has an interesting physiological characteristic where it shows more blue in strongly acidic soil, and red in alkaline soil.[11] Hydrangea, often used as a bouquet flower for weddings, is a flower loved by all generations, both men and women, young and old. There is a hydrangea theme park that spans over 37,000 square meters in Jinam-ri, Dochodo island. Jinam-ri is located under Jangsando Mountain, about 3 km away from the center of Dochodo-myeon.[12]

The park, boasting hydrangeas of exotic atmosphere such as mountain hydrangeas, tree hydrangeas, and Jeju hydrangeas, forms a spectacle in summer with 2 million colorful flowers blooming from about 140,000 hydrangea plants. Dochodo island's Hydrangea Park started in a primary school that was closed in 2005. The hydrangea festival, which first took place in 2019, six years after the residents and Shinan county planted hydrangeas on the abandoned school land and created the park, has established itself as a successful event by word of mouth.[13] In the hydrangea festival held in June 2022, more than 40,000 visitors visited Dochodo island. That's more than ten times the island's population of 3,000. It can't be anything but hopeful news for the island residents, who can't avoid concerns about sustainability due to population decline. Shinan county is currently preparing for the autumn hydrangea festival, planning to hold the country's first autumn hydrangea festival and create a new impetus for flower festivals. In addition, a Pampas Grass Theme Park is also created around Hydrangea Park, adding attractions for the autumn season.

Park Seong-jin, head of the Garden Forestry Department of Shinan county, said the positive effects of the flower festival are not just economic. "About 40,000 people visited the Dochodo island Hydrangea Festival. But even the economic effect is about 1 billion won, it's not just good because outsiders come, but it's better because their children come back, and the children come to the Hydrangea Park to see their parents during the summer vacation. 'Let's go see our hydrangea park. Let's go see our parents.' After people have the hydrangea festival in their hometown of Shinan, 'It's our hometown. Go take a look. It's really good.' This kind of pride in their hometown is the biggest effect."

A common story heard while visiting Shinan county was that there are many people in Bigeumdo island and Dochodo island, that there were many military officials in Bigeumdo and many literary officials in Dochodo. Dochodo High School is still a prestigious school with many students wanting to enter from outside the area and high academic achievements. In the 2018 college entrance exam, all the applicants were successful in early admissions. Dochodo High School was recognized as a

[Figure 2-7] The 2022 Dochodo island Hydrangea Festival visited by over 40,000 tourists

national exemplary case, being selected as one of the 100 outstanding schools in the national curriculum by the Ministry of Education in 2015 due to curriculum innovation. It has also been cited as a successful model of a rural school where about 25% of all students return from inland areas like Mokpo for further education. The success of Dochodo High is deeply related to the long-standing academic enthusiasm of the island residents.

In 1947, the residents of Dochodo island came together to construct a large-scale embankment on the north side of the island through public effort. They organized the Dochodo Neighborhood Council, reorganized 30 natural villages into 10, and shared the responsibility of the embankment construction project by area. The residents themselves were responsible for the construction, and their achievement was the completion of the embankment connecting Hwado village and Oenam-ri. As a result, the Oenam Embankment was completed, within which seven salt pans were created. They named the newly created three salt pans as "School Salt Pans" and donated them as a fund for the establishment of a secondary education institution for the children of the island village. The fund led to the establishment of the Docho High School of Public Citizens (the predecessor of Docho Middle School), which opened in 1952. Students who graduated from elementary school on the island could finally enter secondary education. Considering the oldest age of students at the time of admission was 22, it suggests how long secondary education in the island village had been interrupted. This driving force originated from the island community.[14]

Dochodo island is an island of talents. A stone inscription that reads "The Hometown of Talented People with

Dreams" stands at the entrance of Dochodo island. Of the eight Shinan county mayoral elections, six were won by natives of Dochodo island. The establishment of the school through public effort, which involved the hard labor of the residents, underlies the island's transformation into a cradle of talent. Just as they nurtured talent through their voluntary efforts, they are confident that the future of the island will be opened through the unified strength of the residents. The Hydrangea Festival will be the centripetal force of the residents' unity. Fortunately, the Earth Cultural Facility, created by world-renowned installation artist Olafur Eliasson, will be installed at the summit of the Hydrangea Festival site. It is said that a work symbolizing hydrangeas will also be included, so with the completion of the Earth Cultural Facility, the Hydrangea Festival will certainly attract more attention.

(2) The 10-ri(about 4km) Hackberry Route with K-drama "Woo Young-woo" on Netflix

In 2022, a drama that garnered attention in South Korea, 〈The Strange Lawyer Woo Young-woo〉, featured a Hackberry tree that played a crucial role in preventing the construction of a road in episodes 7 and 8, the 'Sodeok-dong Story.' Starting from a 0.9% viewer rating, it surpassed 15% and became a globally recognized drama. The filming location, Dongbu Village, Daesan-myeon, Uichang-gu, Changwon-si, Gyeongsangnam-do, also buzzed with tourists due to the drama's global popularity, ranking first in the non-English speaking Netflix popularity list. Afterward, several local governments, including Hampyeong county and Boseong county in Jeonnam, began to release press releases saying, "We also have Woo Young-woo's Hackberry tree in our town." On Dochodo island, Shinan county, there is an impressive route of 716 high-quality Hackberry trees and a fantastic garden. The 10-ri(about 4km) Hackberry Route stretches approximately 3.2 km along the waterway from the island's gateway, Hwado pier. 716 Hackberry trees aged 70-100 years form a tunnel on both sides of a cozy walkway.

So how did the 716 Hackberry trees come to Dochodo island? Governor Park Woo-ryang visited Godang-ri, Munnae-myeon, Haenam county several times from 30 years ago and said that the sight of dozens of old Hackberry trees standing along the stream was beautiful. In particular, the sight of the Hackberry trees after their leaves had fallen in the winter was touching. After 2006, Governor Park was looking for a place in Shinan county to create a Hackberry forest road. Jeollanam-do was planning to create an island of safari on Dochodo island and purchased 240,000 pyeong of land from 2013. Since enough land was secured on Dochodo island, they were able to create the beautiful forest road on Dochodo island, which had been dreamed of since 2006. County officials scoured the country to find Hackberry trees. Some came from as far as Hongseong county, Chungcheongnam-do, and Jinju city, Gyeongsangnam-do, but most came from coastal areas of Jeonnam, such as Goheung county, Haenam county, and Jangheung county. The targets were Hackberry trees that casually grew on farm boundaries and shaded crops, or those that took root in mountain slopes or agricultural waterways and were treated poorly.

When rumors spread that the county was collecting old Hackberry trees, there were people who called directly. Inquiries continued about whether they could take trees that were about to be uprooted because they were hindering construction work. A farmer in Jangheung county even called to ask if they could uproot a Hackberry tree that was taking up farmland in the middle of a field. In this way, Hackberry trees from all over the country migrated to Dochodo island. Additionally, with 94 Hackberry trees over 300 years old designated as protected trees by Jeollanam-do and well preserved within Shinan county, Shinan county is the place where you can see more than 810 Hackberry trees in total. When residents heard the news of creating a Hackberry forest road, their initial reaction was lukewarm. There was much opposition because the plan was to buy a field with a width of 16.5 meters and plant trees. Some residents protested, worrying that the shadow would ruin the farming or what to do if flocks of sparrows swarmed in. However, it is said that the residents who were against it did not persist to the end, persuaded that this forest would eventually feed Dochodo island.[15]

Imagine how much budget was spent on finding Hackberry trees and planting them on Dochodo island. Team leader Jang Yu, who has a keen insight into the distribution network information in the landscaping field, proposed donations directly to the tree owners to save the budget. Compared to carrying out the project through a bid to a landscaping company, which costs between 10 million and 30 million won per Hackberry tree, they saved about 80% of the budget by directly paying 10–20% to the tree owner as compensation after receiving a donation. It was possible to reduce the budget, which would have been 24 billion won in total, to about 4 billion won through the amendment of the ordinance for payment after donation. Moreover, when planting through a landscaping company, only the standard of tree height (h) and root diameter (r) need to be passed regardless of the tree shape, so it's harder to get a nice tree than you think. This can be seen as a casc where the budget of a local autonomous entity with

[Figure 2-8] The 10-ri Hackberry Route reflected in Wolpo Stream

a low degree of fiscal independence was maximized through the footwork of public officials who are well aware of the field.

The 716 Hackberry trees donated in this way were loaded onto trucks and arrived at Amtaedo island, then loaded onto boats to arrive at Bigeumdo island Gasan Port. They traveled a long way across the bridge to Dochodo island. Considering that 1-2 trucks were loaded on a small boat and 4 trucks on a large boat, the number of boat operations used for transportation would have been in the hundreds. Wolpo Stream, which flows parallel to the Hackberry forest road, reflects the Hackberry trees, making the forest road even more beautiful. They also plan to launch a ferry in the future, creating a landscape reminiscent of an Oriental painting.

3) Baby Camellias, Crocosmia, and Aphaedo island

The islands of Shinan are divided into the northern region, the central region, and the Hongdo region. Imjado, Jido, Jeungdo, Jaeundo, Amtaedo, Anjwado, Palgeumdo, Jangsando, Sinuido, Hauido, Dochodo, Bigeumdo,

Amtaedo, and Aphaedo islands are representative islands of the northern and central regions.

Among them, the most central island is Aphaedo island, where the county office is located. In 2008, Aphae Bridge was built, connecting it to Mokpo city, and in 2013, it was connected to Muan county through the Kim Dae-jung Bridge, making it feel more like land than an island. Shinan county office also moved here in 2011 after leaving Mokpo, and in 2019, it became the center of the southwest coast as it was connected to Amtaedo island, Jaeundo island, Palgeumdo island, and Anjwado island with the opening of the Cheonsa(1004) Bridge. They are currently working on connecting to Haenam county through Mokpo city. Aphaedo island is truly a transportation hub, as it is not far from Muan International Airport and can directly access the West Coast Expressway.

On Aphaedo island, the central island of Shinan, there is Cheonsa(1004) island Bonsai Park, and inside it is the Evening Glow Art Museum. The Flopia Project and the One Museum Per One island Project are taking place simultaneously, and it plays a role similar to the headquarters of the two projects. Aphaedo Bonsai Park is located on a 10ha site on the southern slope of Songgong Mountain. It is an art park with a bonsai garden, sculpture park, mini arboretum, art museum, and forest bath in a sea garden overlooking the Dado Sea. In 2020, Jeollanam-do even selected it as a premium forest for the Blue Economy that you must visit. It is also a winter tourist spot that forms a flower habitat with about 17,000 baby camellia flowers in red, white, and pink. It takes at least 30 minutes to walk to the observatory on the slope of Songgong Mountain, making it an event road for couples. Banners with embarrassingly sweet phrases like 'Please catch my heart,' 'Don't let go of my hand,' the 'Four Seasons Flowering Flopia island Shinan Mailbox,' and various camellia-related poems here and there make you pause for a moment.[16]

The Baby Camellia Festival at Cheonsa(1004) island Bonsai Park began in 2013, but it was neglected without much attention until it was resumed in 2020 for the second festival. The festival's name is the Aphaedo island Winter Flower Baby Camellia Festival. Unlike the camellia, the baby camellia has hair on the back of young branches and leaves, and the pistil is divided into three. The flowers bloom from November to the following January, in red,

[Figure 2-9] Aphaedo island Bonsai Park with fully bloomed winter baby camellia flowers

[Figure 2-10] The only camellia that blooms in winter, the baby camellia

white, and pink, with white stamens and yellow ovules. It can grow up to 10 meters tall. Baby camellias are planted over 2km in 10ha out of the 20ha of Cheonsa(1004) island Bonsai Park, a scenic spot overlooking the sea. Walking between the baby camellia flowers, which catch the eye with their white and pink hues, one can lose track of time, completely engrossed in the flowers. While regular camellia flowers fall as a whole, baby camellia petals fall apart, creating an illusion of snow falling when the wind blows.[17]

Camellias are generally associated with winter flowers, but actually, camellias do not bloom in winter and bloom from March to April. To be precise, it's called spring camellia. "The only camellia that blooms in winter is the baby camellia, and the formal name of the baby camellia is 'Mountain Flower' because it blooms a lot in the mountains," said Director Park Young-cheol. "The flower mutated into a double flower, so it blooms in winter." Director Park also said that he collected baby camellias from all over the country through donations. "The original design cost was 480,000 won per tree, but when we did it, we bought it for about 60,000 or 70,000 won. We planted more than 20,000

[Figure 2-11] Crocosmia decorating Aphaedo island in summer

[Figure 2-12] Hongdo Lily Festival held in July when lilies are in full bloom

[Figure 2-13] Byeongpungdo island's Mandrake Garden, full of red

[Figure 2-14] Banwol and Bakjido island full of purple with lavender and asters

ten-year-olds, and since we planted about 70,000 throughout Shinan, you can't see as many baby camellias anywhere in the country as you can in Shinan," he said proudly.

Under the white snow that falls softly and invitingly, the shyly blooming baby camellias evoke the image of a young girl just out of adolescence. Walking the baby camellia path during Christmas or the year-end and New Year holidays, when white snow is falling, seems to promise a very romantic scene. Under the baby camellia path, crocosmia flowers were planted and a festival was held in July 2022. The 2 million crocosmia flowers, a perennial flower with beautiful meanings like "innocence" and "I'm still waiting for you", similar to irises, bloom brilliantly with long, oval, reddish-orange flowers in the midsummer of July-August. At the top of the Aphaedo island Cheonsa(1004) island Bonsai Park, covered with baby camellia and crocosmia flowers in winter and summer, there is an observatory where you can see the calm sea of the West Sea. The vast calm sea spread out over 50 million pyeong looks like a garden, and together with the 50,000 pyeong Bonsai Garden, it is called a "Sea Garden" of 50.05 million pyeong.

5. Expanding Flopia and Its Development Direction

As of 2022, there are eight completed gardens in Shinan county. These include Imjado island, where you can see tulips and red camellias; Seondo island, where Narcissus bloom; Byeongpungdo island, the island of red mandrakes; Jaeundo island, full of magnolia flowers; Aphaedo, the heaven of baby camellias; Palgeumdo, blanketed with royal azaleas; Purple island (Banwoldo and Bakjido island), where you can see lavender and other purple flowers; and Dochodo island with its enticing hydrangea park. Each is covered in a single type of flower, ranging in area from 10,000 pyeong(Korean units of measurement, equivalent to 3.3m^2 or 35.5 ft^2) to 130,000 pyeong. Gardens under construction include Jido island, the island of lilacs; Jeungdo island, where you can see Magnolia grandiflora and Pittosporum; Bigeumdo island, the Red Beach island of Rosa rubiginosa; Anjwado island, planted with Melia azedarach; Jangsando, the island of Osmanthus fragrans; Uido island, the island of Daphnes; Okdo island, the island of peonies and magnolias; Maehwado island, the island of pink; and Hauido island, the island of Lonicera japonica and tangerines.

One of the notable upcoming Flopia projects is the olive garden on Sinuido island. As Shodojima near Naoshima in Japan is cited as a successful case of the sixth industry for olive farming and processed product sales, there is expectation about what effect the olive garden on Sinuido will have. Looking at Shinan county's Flopia project, one can easily notice the intense spirit of exploration. They comprehensively grasp the characteristics of an island, choose the flowers and trees optimized for the island, and plant and cultivate them in appropriate locations. For the Flopia project to receive greater response, it needs to consider the following points.

1) Formation of Supporters or Fandom

Currently, the Flopia project can be considered a project led by the local government. It was planned through the initiative of the county mayor who has a special interest in flowers and trees, and the plan is gradually being realized through the efforts of public servants who share the same goal. Of course, it can be seen that flowers and trees are being maintained through the participation of residents. However, there is a cost to engage residents, and as the area expands, the burden on the local government budget increases. Therefore, there is a need to boldly abandon the paradigm of operating the Flopia project with personnel and budget within the local government. It's about attracting people from outside who love flowers and trees. The global success of BTS is due to the existence of the A.R.M.Y., an unparalleled fandom. It is now difficult to depend solely on unilaterally offered content. Efforts are needed to design and organize the participation of recipients, or visitors.

Now is the time to offer the Flopia gardens to people around the world who love flowers, and plan for them to cultivate the gardens themselves, rather than having the local government take the lead in operations. A good benchmarking case can be Sookdo island in Goheung, Jeonnam. The beautiful garden on Sookdo island, started by the couple Go Chae-yoon and Kim Sang-hyun, is gaining popularity thanks to the care of volunteers from outside the village as well as the residents.[18] It's also worth considering boldly entrusting the operation of Shinan county's Flopia garden to outsiders who love flowers and residents of sister cities.

2) Development of Additional Products for Sustainability

It takes a big decision for someone to visit an island to see flowers. They are moved by the sight of beautiful flowers in harmony with nature. However, the reality is that there aren't many additional products to satisfy the hearts of tourists who want to keep their memories. After seeing the flowers, there is a lack of additional elements to satisfy the desire to share the excitement and keep it for a long time. An expansion of the senses is needed to feel the beauty of the flowers seen and smelled with the tongue, ears, and skin. When a subject is perceived through multiple senses, the emotion is doubled and can be remembered for a long time. After seeing the flowers, we need to satisfy the desire to take home flower seeds, bouquets, or flower pots. Instead of just looking at flowers with the eyes, they should experience drinks and food using flowers that can be felt with the tongue. Accommodation should be provided to experience the Flopia Garden in various ways.

A benchmarking case that offers additional experiences to plants is Shodoshima, the Olive island. Not only large-scale olive farms but also various experiential tourism such as olive parks and a variety of processed products such as olive oil, olive pickles, and olive hand cream have been developed and sold to domestic and foreign tourists, establishing itself as an important source of income for the region.[19] In particular, cider and olive ice cream using olives have established themselves as must-try foods among tourists. Such various multi-purposes accumulate economic value on the island, which is essential for a sustainable island. Professor Hiroshi Kakazu, a social economist at Ryukyu University, argued that the introduction of a 'circular economic society' system is needed to maintain a sustainable island economic system by promoting consumption within the island by producing within the island, ultimately preventing goods from leaving the island and resolving the economic deficit.[20] Creating jobs by connecting attractive capital to economic accumulation leads to an influx of people. Therefore, an island inhabited by people will never disappear.

Here Comes The Purple Island

Chapter 3

Art Marketing that Revives a Region with Art

Hong Kyung Soo(Ajou University)

Another noteworthy ambition in Shinan county's plan is art marketing, an effort to inject life into the region through art. It's a daring idea to build a museum on each island. With Shinan county consisting of over 1004 islands, it's a daring plan to build up to 1004 museums. A concrete plan has been set up to establish 24 art museums or museums on 24 islands with a budget of 138.2 billion won.

Will the creation of art museums really help Shinan county's regional regeneration? Such skepticism was easily resolved by the participation of renowned artists from around the world. With the launch of the "One Museum Per One island Project", it's certain that Shinan county's cultural and artistic tourism will enter a new dimension. As of July 2022, 14 museums have already been completed, eight are in progress, and three are in planning. In this chapter, I would like to examine Shinan county's art marketing, which infuses life into the region through art, while introducing representative museums in Shinan county.

1. The Floating Art Museum, Anjwado Island, Commemorating the Artistic Spirit of Kim Whan-ki

It would not be an exaggeration to say that the start of Shinan county's "One Museum Per One Island Project" began with painter Kim Whan-ki. Kim Whan-ki, a world-class artist who was born as the son of a landlord in Eupdong-ri, Anjwa-myeon, and worked in Tokyo, Paris, and New York. He studied at the Art Department of a Japanese university, held five solo exhibitions while residing in Paris, the home of art, from 1956 to 1959, after serving as a professor at Seoul National University. After serving as the Dean of the College of Fine Arts at Hongik University upon returning to Korea, he settled in New York in 1963 as an opportunity to participate in the São Paulo Biennale in Brazil. Although he could not return to his hometown and passed away after living in New York for 11 years, he held eight solo exhibitions, igniting his last flame as an artist.

1) Korea's Top Painter Born in Shinan

There are various adjectives to describe Kim Whan-ki. First and foremost, he is the first Korean painter to surpass 10 billion won in auction, with a record-breaking 13.2 billion won. Nine of the top ten works in the auction price

[Figure 3-1] Floating Museum Designed by Yanagi Yukinori

ranking of Korean modern and contemporary art are his. Docent Jung Woo-chul evaluated him as "Kim Whan-ki is the first abstract painter in Korea, and is a national treasure-class painter called the Picasso of Korea."[1] Indeed, during his residence in Paris, Kim Whan-ki's interest was solely in Picasso, and he understood Picasso's artistic spirit better than anyone else.

Despite being a representative painter of Korean art, unfortunately, there is not a single piece of Kim Whan-ki's work in his birthplace on Anjwado island. It was worrisome what could console the empty hearts of tourists who traveled a long way. On the other hand, many of his works are on display at the Whan-ki Museum in Buam-dong, Seoul. It is too late but natural to establish a museum where you can see Kim Whan-ki's works in his hometown, Anjwado island, where the artist was born, grew up, and formed the roots of the art world. It just so happens that the Shinan county office has a collection of 31 of Kim Whan-ki's paintings. You can check the list on the county office's website.[2] There are series of prints made in his Paris workshop, flowers and jars, sketches, Yokohama landscapes, moon and jar, figure point view, fish, full moon, mountain moon, etc. In particular, 'Birthplace Landscape' is a work that depicts the artist's birthplace in Anjwado island through the artist's eyes, which fits well with the museum to be introduced in Anjwado island.

There were plans to build a Kim Whan-ki Art Museum on Anjwado island, but the process of discussions with stakeholders was not smooth and was even frustrated. Now, instead of a museum commemorating Kim Whan-ki, they are planning to build a 'floating museum' on the water, which will be located near the old house of Kim Whan-ki in Eupdong-ri, Anjwa-myeon, at Sinchon Reservoir. Five permanent exhibition halls in the shape of a cube, one planned exhibition hall, and one office floating on the water boast outstanding sculptural qualities on their own. The museum's design, which reflects four surfaces of the cubic shape on the water, was undertaken by Yanagi Yukinori, who designed the Seirensho Art Museum on Inujima, one of Naoshima's art islands. The floating museum, transformed into a new art museum by Yanagi Yukinori, who had turned an abandoned copper refinery into an art space opened in 2024.

2) Whan-ki Blue Capturing the Sea and Sky of Anjwado island

How would the painter Kim Whan-ki feel if he knew that a museum honoring him was being built in his hometown of Anjwado island? Kim Whan-ki was a very creative artist who not only painted but also devoted himself to writing and had various cultural ambitions such as urban planning. He wanted to plan the city of Seoul with a compass and a ruler, and if that was not possible, he wanted to remodel a building so that the lower floor was made into a pure art museum to hold a craftwork exhibition, the second floor into a craft art factory to produce living arts, and the third floor into an art research institute where excellent young artists gather, to create a comprehensive art production building.[3)] It can be speculated that he could have been active as a Minister of Culture if he had lived healthily in Korea. Would not the cultural powerhouse Korea have been completed earlier?

He also imagined turning Ui-dong into a cultural village, having all the artworks produced in the cultural village sold under the responsibility of the government, adding a cultural tax to the national tax to support artists, and a welfare system. In the 1950s, he wanted to build an art museum himself in about 20 years. He imagined the location to be deep in the mountains, with free admission, but sold painting books.[4]

His paintings contain a lot of thoughts about his hometown and the sea. There is no doubt that his longing for his hometown became more earnest after graduating from junior high school in Japan and entering the art department of a Japanese university. He reproduced the landscape in his memory and won an award at the 'Igwajeon' in Japan in the fall of 1935. The work he submitted to the

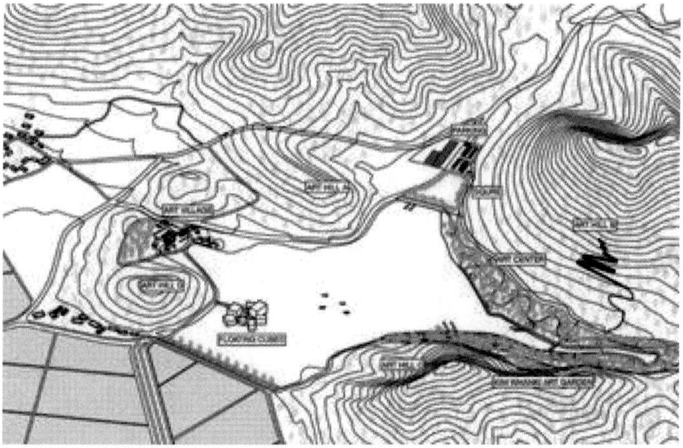

[Figure 3-2] Kim Whan-ki's birthplace village in Anjwado island to be reborn as an art town

gateway to recognition as a formal painter in Japan was a lyrical depiction of the everyday landscape of Shinan. This work titled ⟨When the Bush Warbler Sings⟩ is a painting of an extremely southern region where a girl wearing a jacket and skirt appears, and clouds, birch trees, and bird eggs are depicted. "I was born and raised on a warm island in the south. The island was peaceful until the typhoon came. However, it was especially my hometown where, when the bush warbler started singing in spring, I would feel things that I didn't know whether I was alive or dead, anyway, I just felt something I didn't know (May 1956)."[5]

Could the 'things he did not know' not be the beauty of the sea, wind, and sunshine of Anjwado island? His paintings are full of blue. Critics believe that the blue, called 'Whan-ki Blue', came from the sea and sky of his hometown, Anjwado island. The records and impressions of his hometown are profound in his writings. "My hometown is Anjwado island, Jeonnam. From the doorway of our house in my hometown, you can see Yudalsan in Mokpo across the sea. It is an island that you can reach in two hours by taking a hundred-horsepower putt-putt boat from Mokpo port across a lake-like sea. It is just a dreamlike island, a dreamlike hometown. It is an island where snow quietly piles up in winter and a seasonal wind passes once in summer, and it is about a day's walk from end to end because its length and width are similar. When friends ask, 'How big is your hometown island?' I answer, 'We can't play soccer on our island.' Because it seems like the ball will fall into the sea if you kick it. Still, on the island, there are plains that produce thousands of stones, and mountains that are layered, and there are waterfalls that combine twelve valleys. Beautiful blue pines are densely packed in the gentle Ansan village, and in the past, ginseng used to grow, but now deodeok and pine mushrooms grow in heaps. When I look at the mountain densely filled with pine trees that have fallen, and think of myself who grew up in that mountain, the thought of my hometown is just the thought of Ansan... This spring, the island girls will probably dig up bracken and shepherd's purse on the sunny hillside."[6]

Kim Whan-ki, who struggled fiercely with art all his life and passed away in New York without being able to return to his homeland. His beloved hometown Anjwado island intends to remember him by building an art museum that can commemorate Kim Whan-ki's artistic spirit. Fans who love him will now be able to appreciate the mesmerizing color of Whan-ki Blue while looking at the sky, sea, and land of Anjwado island.

"I am an Eastern person, a Korean, and no matter how much I change, I cannot do anything beyond my ideal. My painting is a painting of an Eastern person, and it can only be a painting of a thorough Korean. Shouldn't the most nationalistic be the most global? I left our country and knew more about our country, expressed it, and thought about it. Art is the song of a powerful nation. Coming to the stage called Paris, our sky looked more powerful, and our song sounded powerful."[7] Just like the title of his work "In the evening"(1969), you will now be able to meet Kim Whan-ki in pictures on Anjwado island.

"Among so many stars out there,
A single star gazes upon me.
Among so many people here,
I gaze upon hat single star.
As the night deepens,
The star disappears into the brightness,

And I vanish into the darkness.

How precious we are,

You, the one, and me, the one,

Where and what shall we become

And meet again."

The poet Kim Kwang-seob, a friend of Kim Whan-ki who resided in New York, sent a magazine containing his poetry to Kim Whan-ki. After reading it, Kim Whan-ki was inspired to create a masterpiece. The countless dots that make up Kim Whan-ki's paintings are likely the islands of the Dado Sea, gradually filling the Anjwado island Sea that he longed to see. Perhaps it is so.

2. Infinito Museum in Jaeundo island

On the resort island of Jaeundo, the Infinito Museum is being constructed through a collaboration between the artist Park Eun-sun, active in Italy, and Swiss architect Mario Botta. The museum is scheduled to be completed in the spring of 2025. I learned about the construction of the

Infinito Museum from Kim Yoon, the director of Mokpo MBC. Shinan county narrowly secured the museum of Park Eun-sun, which was about to move to another city. How did a world-renowned sculptor's museum end up being built in Shinan county? The story goes like this.

1) Why was it built in Shinan, not in Busan or Mokpo?

A few years ago, Sculptor Park Eun-sun was invited by the city of Busan to exhibit his works. Former Busan Mayor Seo Byoung-soo, who carefully examined Park Eun-sun's sculptures, suggested to Park that they create a museum in

[Figure 3-3] Aerial View of the Infinito Museum, a collaboration between a world-renowned architect and sculptor

Busan, a proposal that Park is known to have accepted. The Infinito Museum was nearly established in Busan. However, with Mayor Seo's failure to be re-elected and the change of mayors, the plan to build the museum in Busan fell through.

Mario Botta, known as the architect of the soul, is a Swiss architect known for designing religious buildings. He has designed buildings in major cities around the world and is known in Korea for designing the Gangnam Kyobo Tower and the Samsung Leeum Museum. Botta promised to design a museum in a location of Park's choice, maintaining a close relationship with the artist. After much consideration, Park suggested a location near Seoul, accessible to many people. Botta advised, "Your work cannot but be influenced by the hometown where you were born. How about establishing it in your hometown?" Park decided to meet with the Mayor of Mokpo, and in this process, the role was taken by Kim Yoon, the director of Mokpo MBC and a high school junior of Park. Upon hearing the news of Park's visit to Mokpo from Director Kim, Shinan county governor Park Woo-ryang requested a meeting with Park before his interview with the Mayor of Mokpo. Thus, a meeting between

Governor Park and Artist Park took place. Governor Park proposed the following to Artist Park.

"If your hometown is Mokpo, and the Mayor of Mokpo, whom you will meet, proposes to build a museum in Mokpo, then let's do so. But if there's no such proposal from Mokpo City, let's build a museum in Shinan county." There was no proposal for the establishment of a museum from Mokpo City. Upon hearing this news, Governor Park immediately took Artist Park to Shinan county. After the survey, the site was decided to be near Dunjang beach on Jaeundo island. Mario Botta visited Jaeundo island several times for the design and began construction once the design was completed. If everything goes as planned, the Infinito Museum will be completed in 2025 and will attract numerous tourists. Director Kim Yoon fantasized about having a celebratory performance by Andrea Bocelli, a close friend of Artist Park, at the museum's opening ceremony. If all great achievements are the result of imagination, the delightful imagination of hearing Bocelli's "Time to Say Goodbye" on the beach of Jaeundo island also seems likely to become a reality.

2) The Artistic World of Sculptor Park Eun-sun

In the spring of 2022, a collaboration between Park Eun-sun and tenor Andrea Bocelli became a hot topic. On July 28, 2022, news reported the installation of a large marble sculpture titled 'Infinite Column,' 11 meters high and weighing 22 tons, on the stage of Bocelli's concert in Lajatico, Tuscany, Italy. Bocelli named the concert title 'Infinite (Infinito),' and the title of Park's sculpture is also

[Figure 3-4] The first exhibition of sculptor Park Eun-sun on island day

Infinite Column (Colonna Infinit). The similarity in the names of the concert and the sculpture shows how captivated Bocelli was by the spirituality and theme contained in Park Eun-sun's abstract sculpture. Bocelli reportedly took the title from the sculpture to harmonize classical performances and art.

How on earth did Park Eun-sun and Andrea Bocelli become intertwined, sharing artistic inspiration? Bocelli, after feeling Park Eun-sun's abstract sculpture with his hands and appreciating the work with his heart's eyes, gave a review that it was 'the best work that leads to deep meditation.' In the summer of 2021, when Park Eun-sun held an outdoor sculpture exhibition on the beach at the invitation of the famous Tuscan resort city Viareggio, Bocelli suggested installing sculptures at his own beach club. As a result, Park Eun-sun was able to successfully hold an outdoor exhibition in Viareggio. This led to Bocelli requesting that Park set up a sculpture at his concert, resulting in a collaboration between music and art. Given this close relationship, it doesn't seem impossible for Bocelli to perform at the opening ceremony of the Infinito Museum.

After graduating from Kyunghee University's College of Art, Artist Park graduated from the Carrara Academy of Fine Arts, famous for marble for sculpture, and has been active in Pietrasanta, the hometown of world sculpture art, since 1993. He has been praised for his simple yet constructive abstract works that combine the profound and subtle spirituality of the East with the sculptural language of the West. He has held solo exhibitions at the invitation of various cities and museums in Europe and has been actively working around the world. Currently, more than 20

[Figure 3-5] Bocelli's concert poster using Park Eun-sun's 'Infinite Column'

public sculptures by Park Eun-sun are installed in various cities in Italy and Europe.

In particular, in 2016, he held a large-scale outdoor exhibition for three months, displaying 14 sculptures in various places such as the Piazza Michelangelo, which overlooks the city of Florence, Italy, the Palazzo Vecchio, Piazza Pitti, and the airport. Dario Nardella, the mayor of Florence who invited Park Eun-sun to hold a sculpture exhibition at the time, praised, "I am pleased to install Park

[Figure 3-6] Bocelli singing in front of Park Eun-sun's sculpture (Italy, July 28, 2022)

Eun-sun's excellent works that encapsulate the aesthetics of Eastern and Western art in various parts of Florence." After studying in Italy, he received an offer to become a university professor in his home country, but instead of a comfortable and stable path, he devoted himself to working as a full-time artist in the hometown of sculpture, and emerged as a representative sculptor in Europe. Currently, Park Eun-sun is an exclusive artist of the Contini Gallery in Italy and is known as the sculptor with the most prolific works and the most active exhibition activities in Italy.

In 2018, Park Eun-sun received the prestigious 'Fratelli Rosselli' award, given by the city of Pietrasanta to the artist who has achieved the most outstanding accomplishment in the field of sculpture. In 2021, in recognition of his artistic achievements, he became the first Asian to become an honorary citizen of Pietrasanta. Moreover, this year, he permanently installed a large-scale work, 'Infinite Column', at the entrance rotary of the highway, at the request of the city. The number of sculptors who have installed their works in public places in Pietrasanta can be counted on one hand, including Fernando Botero (Colombia) and Igor Mitoraj (Poland), so it can be said to be a great achievement in the Korean contemporary sculpture world.

In an interview with NewsPim, Park Eun-sun confessed, "In the early days, I would work in a corner of the studio even though I was about to be kicked out because I was running out of boarding money. I had nowhere else to go. One Sunday morning, a couple of collectors who happened to be on a studio tour took a closer look at my work and found me still working in the evening, and bought the work on the spot. I was on the brink of a cliff, but I dramatically overcame the crisis. Since then, there have been many desperate moments, but I have continued to advance without hesitation, and now I have achieved the goal that every sculptor working in this city most wishes for: the permanent installation of a work in Pietrasanta."[8]

The installation of an 11-meter-tall large-scale sculpture by Park Eun-sun at the entrance of the highway leading to this world-renowned sculpture city has several implications. It is a comprehensive evaluation of the originality and artistry of Park Eun-sun's work, as well as his achievements in Tuscany, Italy. The world of Park Eun-sun's work, recognized from the sacred site of global sculpture, will now unfold on Jaundo island, a resort island. It is scheduled to open in May 2025.

3) The Architectural World of Mario Botta

Mario Botta was born in Mendrisio, Switzerland, in 1943. After an apprenticeship in Lugano, he graduated from the Milan School of Art and the Venice School of Architecture. While studying in Venice, he had the opportunity to work for Le Corbusier and Louis Kahn. He designed the Church of San Giovanni Battista in Mogno, Switzerland, the Evry Cathedral in Evry, France, the San Francisco Museum of Art (SFMOMA), and the Tinguely Museum in Basel, Switzerland, and won the Swiss Architecture Award.

His architectural philosophy, as presented on his website, encompasses eight elements: the context of the location, the historicity of the city, light, gravity, geometry/symmetry/order, natural materials, respect for the past and memory, and ethics over aesthetics.[9] If we were to summarize his philosophy, it would be sculptural stability and a socio-ethical attitude. Sculptural stability includes light, gravity, geometry/symmetry/order, while socio-ethical attitude includes the context of the location, the historicity of the city, natural materials, respect for memory, and ethics. Therefore, his architecture appears calm, stable, and devoid of superfluous elements.

Mario Botta designed several iconic landmark buildings in Korea. The most representative of these is the Kyobo Tower, a reddish-brown brick building at Gangnam Kyobo intersection. The importance of the site, light, geometry, and natural materials are among the key elements of Mario Botta's architectural philosophy. In particular, the reason for using brick as a construction material corresponds to the natural materials in his architectural philosophy. It is said to be made from a natural material, earth, and therefore has good durability. Perhaps due to the characteristics of the reddish-brown brick material, Kyobo Tower appears calm and serious, boasting an aesthetic that subtly asserts its presence without ostentation. By finishing an otherwise ordinary rectangular building with just red bricks, it not only provides material contrast and visual intensity compared to the surrounding colorless or glass buildings, but also gives the building itself a sense of weight. If you find yourself wanting to visit Kyobo Bookstore every time you pass by Gangnam in Seoul, that's the power of Mario

Botta's architectural philosophy.

Mario Botta's work can also be found at the Leeum Museum in Hannam-dong, Seoul, where his architecture stands alongside buildings designed by Rem Koolhaas and Jean Nouvel. The most noticeable among them is a red brick building designed by Mario Botta, which is in the shape of an inverted cone. The inverted conical building and the fortress-like structure, reminiscent of European castles, differentiate it from the other two buildings in Leeum in terms of form, while its distinctive red brick offers a strong visual impact. Inside the building, there is a spiral staircase that maintains the exterior shape of the building. The ceiling of the central interior space is made of glass,

[Figure 3-7] Mario Botta, who visited Jaeundo island several times to design the Infinito Museum

allowing natural light to reach the underground lobby. This light, along the white interior walls and through the windows along the spiral staircase, offers a glimpse into Mario Botta's architectural philosophy on light. Mario Botta described the Leeum Museum as follows: "This building is a space with a ceramic art museum in mind. I wanted to create a mysterious form that magnified a ceramic vase. It's about making someone passing through the city want to come into the museum because of its mysterious appearance."[10]

The third well-known building in Korea is the Cathedral in Shrine of Our Lady of the Rosary of Namyang, which was completed in 2020. This is the most recent project that Mario Botta has undertaken in Korea, and it is said to have been completed after 14 rounds of design revisions over eight years, travelling back and forth between Korea and Switzerland. While Botta has designed a variety of buildings, he has received particular attention for his religious architecture. He is one of the few architects who has designed buildings for various religions, including Christianity, Islam, and Judaism. His religious architecture extends beyond stereotypical designs to creative ones, encompassing deep contemplation about the perception of religion, the influence that religious architecture will have in the future, and its symbolism. "I want to build a building that meets the spiritual needs of humans beyond the material."[11] The Cathedral became a topic of conversation when the documentary "Mario Botta: Architecture for the Soul" was released in 2020. The Shrine of Our Lady of the Rosary of Namyang Cathedral, which also uses red bricks as its main exterior material, catches the eye with its two cylindrical towers, a sight not commonly seen in traditional cathedral architecture. The light flowing in through the gap between the two towers creates a spiritual space inside, and the building, acting as a 'fence' on the ground in the valley, was intended to create a space where the soul is healed, separated from the complicated world. This is probably why he is called 'the architect of the soul'.[12]

The Infinito Museum plans to display works by various artists, but the main works will be those of sculptor Park Eun-sun. Therefore, the Infinito Museum designed by Mario Botta is expected to be a building that uses a lot of marble. The Infinito Museum, to be erected right in front of Dunjang beach on Jaeundo island, is expected to be another work of art born from the collaboration of world-renowned artists, boasting an excellent sea view, and is likely to become the core base of "the One Museum Per One Island Project" in Shinan county. The Infinite Bridge, which is connected to Dunjang beach, was also named by the artist Park Eun-sun, and the fact that it is noted in Italian probably takes into account the artist's stage of activity. If you walk to Halmido island after visiting the museum, feeling the sea breeze and walking on the sea, the journey will be more than worth it. Currently, many tourists are visiting, drawn by the name, now called the Infinito Bridge (Bridge of Infinity). The Ramada Hotel & Sea One Resort in Jaeundo island, which was completed in 2022, features works by Lee Lee-nam, one of Korea's top media artists. The works themed on Jaeundo island, 'Waterfall of Grace' and works featuring waves are impressive.

3. Sea Art Museum in Bigeumdo Island and Antony Gormley

The Sea Art Museum is being built on Bigeumdo island,

and it is planned to feature the work of world-renowned installation artist Antony Gormley. Gormley's work is filled with pathos that shakes the bodies and minds of visitors. When I heard that Gormley's work was coming to Shinan county, I doubted my ears. I was very curious about who the planner was who had the audacious imagination to bring in the work of Gormley, one of the greatest installation artists of our time.

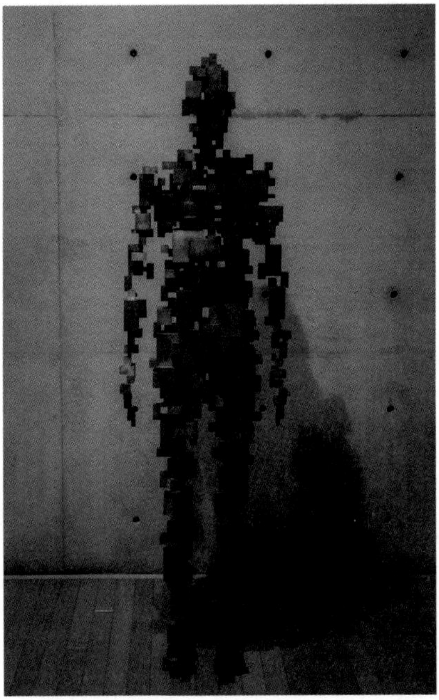

[Figure 3-8] Antony Gormley's <Sublimate IV>, with a chilly sadness

A few years ago, I had the opportunity to spend a night at the Benesse House, a lodge designed by Tadao Ando, when I visited Naoshima. I enjoyed the feel of Ando's touch inside the accommodation, but in the end, I couldn't sleep. Art causes ripples in the hearts of indifferent people. After tossing and turning all night, I went out into the hallway. Suddenly, I discovered a statue, Gormley's work 〈Sublimate IV〉. I was coldly shocked to see the figure of a human body shattered and crystallized into small pixels. Although it was a lump of small cubes with no discernible expression or complexion, I could strongly feel what kind of emotion it was experiencing. Just like the title 'Sublimate', I faintly felt the hollow body of a person who could not express their desire and sublimated into something else. I vaguely realized that Gormley is a sculptor who draws human emotions with human-like figures. So who is Antony Gormley?

He is a sculptor born in the UK in 1950. From 1968 to 1971, he majored in archaeology and anthropology at Cambridge University, and then began his path as an artist during three years of meditation in India. For the past 40 years, Gormley has been exploring the relationship between the human body and the spaces we live in. He is famous for his installations such as 〈Angel of the North〉 installed in the coal mining city of Gateshead in 1998, 〈Another Place〉, a collection of 100 human figure sculptures installed on the Crosby beach in Liverpool, 〈Horizon Fields〉, a project of 100 human figure sculptures installed throughout the mountains in Bregenz, Austria, and the 〈Event Horizon〉 series, which involves placing human sculptures on buildings and streets throughout London and New York. His work 〈One & Other〉, where people were exhibited for 24 hours a day for 100 days, changing every hour, on the plinth in Trafalgar Square in London in 2009, was a topic of discussion worldwide.

Gormley gained attention for his unique approach of wrapping his body in a wrap, casting a plaster model, and then casting iron to create a figure. In an interview with art consultant Choi Sun-hee, Gormley said that most of his work was made through live casting (the process of standing still until the plaster hardens and the mold can be removed after plastering the whole body), and that our minds go further when our physical freedom is restricted. It may sound like a paradox, but it is also the basic principle of meditation.

He explained his work logic by saying, "Through live casting, I intentionally limit the range of movement and the ability to express freely, and by willingly giving up all control of the body, I experience moving to a more free space."

This work logic is closely related to his study of archaeology and anthropology, and his three-year experience of meditation in India. After graduating from university, he lived with a monk in India and meditated all the time, which he said was a process of realizing the

[Figure 3-9] Antony Gormley's <Another Place> installed on the coast of central England

correlation between human mind and body. He wanted to express his experiences in India in visual language, and said that it was an important moment in his life that suggested a way forward as an artist.[13]

Looking at the silhouette of the sculpture I saw in Naoshima, Gormley's body is faintly drawn. The human completed as an object and the soul contained within it make the viewer think about time and space, life and humans. What time is it now? Where am I? Who am I and how long will I live? What are my worries and depressions? There are no words that directly point to thoughts in Gormley's works. The shapes he creates only provoke thoughts.

In the fall of 2021, during a lecture on the subject of 'Video Copywriting' conducted with Ajou University students, there was a practice of unfolding stories after showing photos. I chose Gormley's work. It's 〈Another Place〉, completed in 1997. On the Crosby beach on the central west coast of England, Gormley installed 100 human sculptures looking at the sea over a distance of 3 km. As it's a beach with a large tidal range, the sculptures are submerged in water and then revealed as the tide comes in and out. One student Park Ha-yeon left the following passage.

"The graveyard of things that have served their purpose and are left as shells. If not tightly bound and empty, they would fly away in the wind. Who are those who have taken away your essence and left you behind? What was inside you? You who are bound again are now the property of another. I pity you, who have never once had freedom. Things defined only by their utility. No different from anyone else. The grave of the 21st century youth."

I was proud of the student who extracted the language of 'the graveyard of things that have served their purpose and are left as shells without ever having freedom' from the photo of Gormley's work. If such poignant language can come from a photo of Gormley's work, I wonder how much more wonderful ekphrasis (the expression of a picture in writing) would be born when seeing the work in person at the actual site.

Another of Gormley's works that evokes a cool sadness might be ⟨Wasteman⟩. Margate, a southeastern port city near the Dover Strait in the UK, has been a famous resort since the Middle Ages, but it has repeatedly declined since

[Figure 3-10] <Wasteman>, a performance of burning a giant figure of discarded furniture

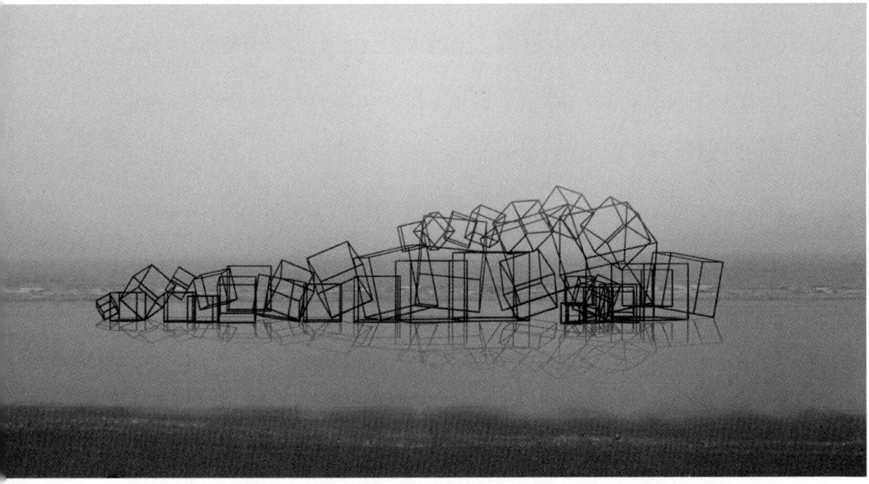

[Figure 3-11] A schematic diagram of Antony Gormley's 'Maritime Cultural Facility'

the 20th century. Gormley collected 30 tons of flammable furniture from inside the houses with the villagers and made a 27-meter-high giant sculpture. Over six weeks, the process of collecting furniture and setting up the statue was designed as a performance that united the residents through the efforts of volunteers composed of residents. Then, at dusk, they set fire to the giant figure made of wooden trash while the residents watched.

The sight of a huge giant burning in flames, emitting smoke, was devastating. The image of it silently enduring and disappearing despite being on fire is preserved in a video. Why did Gormley, who has been doing metal casting work, collect wood and set it on fire? Gormley's intention is as follows. "In a word, the work was an expression of the opening of a new era due to the end of the old age. By incinerating the trash of our lives and discarded objects, I wanted to gain new energy. It also contained the hope of returning from a modern consumer society where everything is excessively mass-produced to an era where the value of the individual was important."[14] In July 2022, Gormley personally visited the site of the Sea Art Museum in Bigeumdo island, Shinan county. While traveling to Bigeumdo island and looking around the Sea Art Museum installation sites, Gormley admired that the nature of Shinan county was so well preserved and also said it was more beautiful than the island of Capri in Italy. Gormley spoke about the significance of installing his work in Shinan county as follows. "Although Shinan county is an island separated from the mainland and transportation is inconvenient, I decided to install the work in Bigeumdo island, Shinan county, thinking that it is more meaningful to give inspiration and healing to someone visiting here by blending my work with the beautifully preserved natural environment than showing my work to many people." If Gormley's work enters Bigeumdo island in Shinan county, it's intriguing to think about how it will harmonize with the beautiful beachfront and uplift us. The opening is scheduled for May 2024.

4. Architectural Art of Seomtiago Pilgrimage Road in Gijeom-Soakdo Island

The following is a story heard from Suh Myung-sook, the

director who created the Jeju Olle trails. When she quit her job as the editor-in-chief of a current affairs magazine and walked the Camino de Santiago in Spain, she was so amazed by the trail that a foreigner walking with her said, "If you like it so much, why don't you create one in your hometown?" This inspired her. She immediately thought of the beautiful hometown trail of Seogwipo, and soon started to create the Olle. The birth of the Olle trail is a major event that shifted the axis of Jeju travel. It is a revolution in travel that has changed from a superficial trip that stays in large hotels and condos centered on the Seogwipo tourist complex, and quickly visits only designated tourist spots such as Yongduam, Samseonghyeol, Seongsanpo, and Hamdeok Beach, to individual trips that delve into the heart of Jeju and stay in private homes.

The Olle craze led to a walking boom, and the number of people who visit Jeju every week, walk a certain section, and return increased. Director Suh Myung-sook said that the happiest thing after creating the Olle trail was that hotel and resort cleaning workers, who had no choice but to rest during the tourist off-season in winter, were able to keep working because tourists did not stop all year round. In this way, the trail brings people, creates jobs, and brings new vitality. Other local governments benchmarked and hundreds of trails were born nationwide. This is the butterfly effect brought about by the Olle trail.

1) Why do trails attract people?

What exactly is a trail that attracts people? Our lives explain it. As of July 2022, over 90% of Koreans live in cities. Life in a crowded city is stressful in itself. Each individual with their own needs, desires, and ambitions moves their eyes to realize their desires. The problem is that because desires are generally similar, collisions are inevitable. The dense presence of others surrounding one can easily exert pressure. Moreover, the pressure from human relationships that arise within the organization one belongs to is never less. People who are easily pressured and hurt by others live in cities.

The easiest way to reduce pressure is walking. In her book "Wanderlust: A History of Walking", Rebecca Solnit explains why walking is an attractive way of life by retracing its history. "The best way to do nothing is to pretend to do something, and the closest thing to doing nothing is walking. Of all the deliberate actions of a human being, walking is the closest thing to the involuntary rhythm of the body (breathing, heartbeat). Walking is a subtle balance between working and not working, just existing and accomplishing something."[15]

According to Solnit, when we walk, we can unfold our thoughts without being lost in them, and walking gives birth to thoughts. Also, passing through a landscape is an echo and stimulant of passing through a thought, and a thought that comes to mind may be part of the landscape that the

[Figure 3-12] House of Matthew, resembling a Greek Orthodox building

mind has passed through. Ultimately, thinking may be more of a matter of passing somewhere than creating something, and for things to happen in the mind, movement of the body and something for the eyes to see are needed. In the end, walking is a means and a destination, and a journey and a destination at the same time.[16]

More than anything, the reason why walking is attractive to modern people is because walking is slow. Escaping from the busy urban life, walking is the best way to leisurely look back at oneself and organize one's mind, and has risen to the top as the best means of healing.

2) Who created the architectural art pilgrimage on Gijeom-Soakdo island?

Gijeom-Soakdo island in Shinan county, Jeonnam, is a small island with 108 residents. It was the island that was most at risk of regional extinction due to population decline and aging. However, since the pilgrimage was created, tourists have been flocking in, and people who had left their hometown are returning. In 2021, 53,000 tourists, an average of 145 per day, more than the number of residents, visited the island. Compared to when there were almost no tourists, it's a great change. The island has revived. Who on earth created this 'Seomtiago'[17] pilgrimage ('Seom' means an island in Korean)? From now, we need to remember that name.

In Jeollanam-do, South Korea, the 'Island We Want to Go' project was set as a brand policy, and six islands were selected as target areas. In April 2015, through a public competition, Ms. Yoon Mi-sook, an island planning specialist who led the creation of the Dongpirang Mural Village in Tongyeong city, Gyeongnam, was appointed as a special committee member for the islands of Jeollanam-do. Gijeom-Soakdo island were selected for Jeollanam-do's 'Island We Want to Go' project in 2018, and the idea of creating an architectural art pilgrimage came through the idea of Specialist Yoon Mi-sook. Initially, Specialist Yoon visited Gijeom-Soakdo island and was at a loss as to how to develop an island that was only a mudflat, but after communicating with the villagers, she decided to start by creating a pilgrimage and a small chapel because most of them were church members. Specialist Yoon communicated with the residents with the thought, 'The ultimate goal is to make the island residents happy while not harming the culture and ecology of the island that has been preserved while being cut off from the mainland, and I want to create not only an island we want to go to but also an island we want to live on.'

Drawing on the fact that the mudflat path is likened to Moses's miracle and 90% of the island residents attend church, she decided to create a pilgrimage named after Jesus's 12 Apostles.[18]

The selected artists include six famous domestic artists: Kim Yun-hwan, Lee Won-seok, Park Young-kyun, Son Min-a, Kang Young-min, Kim Kang, and four foreign

[Figure 3-13] Specialist Yoon Mi-sook, who planned the Seomtiago pilgrimage

artists: Yorai Abraham Shoval, Bruno Pruner, and Yaluk Mass. They lived on the island for a year and created their works. Starting with the first chapel in Dae-Gijeom island (Bigger particle island of Gijeom), they completed the Korean version of the pilgrimage, which spans 12km, including five places in Dae-Gijeom island, two in So-Gijeom island (Smaller particle island of Gijeom), one on the path between So-Gijeom island and Soakdo island, one on Soakdo island, two on Jin island, and one on Ddan island.

[Figure 3-14] The artists who completed the construction and surveyed the Seomtiago pilgrimage

3) A Not-So-Smooth Process

However, the process of creating the path and building the church was not smooth. The five islands each fiercely argued to install central facilities such as guest houses on their respective islands. In November 2018, it was temporarily decided to cancel the project because it was impossible to reconcile opinions among the island residents. Upon receiving the report, county governor Park Woo-ryang called about 14 representative residents of the five islands to his office. To the attending residents, he said, "Everyone who participated today must say everything they want to say to each other and can't go home until their opinions are unified," and closed the door to his office. The meeting, which started around 3 pm, ended around 9 pm when the attendees requested a meeting with Governor Park. When the residents promised to follow the decision of Shinan county, the project found a breakthrough. They promised that if anyone caused trouble over the same issue in the future, they would have to leave the island. All attendees signed a pledge, and the project resumed.

Securing land to install the buildings created by the artists emerged as another issue. The landowners refused to provide the land where the buildings were to be located because it had a good view. Governor Park visited the five islands with his staff and resolved the issue by individually meeting with the landowners to exchange for other lands or promising priority support for county assistance projects to those who provided the land. The project was able to proceed smoothly.

When Governor Park learned that Yoon Mi-sook, a specialist who provided the idea for the Seomtiago project, planned to return to her hometown Tongyeong after finishing her work in Jeollanam-do, he earnestly asked Governor Kim Young-rok and Specialist Yoon Mi-sook, and invited Specialist Yoon as the head of the 'island We Want to Go' promotion team in Shinan county. The project was completed in a direction that matched its original intention.

4) Silence and Tranquility, and the Beauty of Brilliant Harmony

In February 2022, I planned a Seomtiago trip with about

10 members of the Good Country Cooperative, but I, the planner, could not participate because a family member contracted COVID-19. The photos sent by the members via KakaoTalk were so beautiful that I felt sick with envy. Looking at the photos they posted from Seoul, I couldn't feel even a fraction of the sensation of the trip just by imagining it. As soon as July 2022 began, I set out on a field trip to Seomtiago with my 20-something niece, San, who came from Australia. After arriving in Mokpo city the day before and staying at the Mokpo city 1935 Hanok guest house, we set off to catch the 9:30 am ferry departing from Songgong port in Aphaedo island. The dozen tourists gathered at Songgong port for the pilgrimage site investigation could not hide their excitement. I was going to bring a car, but gave up after reading a plea from the locals at the ticket office asking not to bring a car.

The ferry we boarded, Today Ferry 2, seemed to be an old ship that was over 50 years old. It was a ro-ro ship capable of carrying 73 people and about 20 cars with a tonnage of 99t. I thought it should be decommissioned as soon as possible and a new ship should be built. As I was momentarily troubled by worry, the ship departed and passed under the Cheonsa(1004) Bridge. Passing under the towering bridge gave a great aesthetic satisfaction. We savored the sea breeze and blue waves while tasting the sandwiches and salad prepared for us by CEO An Chi-yoon. If only the ship had been better, it would have been an experience not inferior to a Mediterranean cruise. The ship sailing in the shallow sea repeatedly approached and bypassed the nearby islands. A few travelers disembarked when we reached the first island, Soakdo, and the ship made several more stops before reaching Dae-gijeomdo island (Bigger particle island of Gijeom). We saw the first building, the House of Pedro, reminiscent of Santorini in Greece. Against the backdrop of the mud flats, the blue sky spread out, and in front of it, the white and cobalt blue chapel shone brilliantly. After taking commemorative photos, we immediately rented an electric bicycle and started the trip. We went 900M further to the House of Andrea, and then rushed to the House of Jacob. It was impressive that a bench with a red roof was placed next to the architectural art. It seemed like a thoughtful design to place it in a location where weary pilgrims could rest and carefully examine the architecture or nature. Each time a traveler encounters a building, they encounter a new landscape and become immersed in new thoughts.

5) The Boundary Between Kitsch and Beauty

We headed towards the Byeongpungdo island road with the open path. The houses painted with the red color of mandrami, reminiscent of rooster's feathers, came as a shock. The blue sky, green rice fields, and somewhat bright maroon gates and roofs contrasted. We climbed up the towering mandrami garden behind the village and saw the wide mudflats. The newly created village through someone's curation did not feel awkward. From the villagers' point of view, the village became brighter and more cheerful, and the arrival of tourists seemed to evoke pride. The successful color painting, which could seem awkward, appeared to be due to the 'intention' and 'bold' attempt. The clear intention seemed to be 'administration to improve the quality of life for residents', and the bold attempt was manifested in the unity of painting the entire village in the same color without hesitation.

Installing artificial public art in the midst of intact nature can be a risky venture. This is because it can push the beauty of nature far into the background and only the sensual prominence of artificial objects can stick out sharply. In such cases, it is evaluated as 'kitschy'. Kitsch is a term for low-grade artwork, said to have been used to describe cliche paintings produced collectively for tourists who came to Italy in the late 19th century. According to Adorno, kitsch is "what used to be beauty, but has become

[Figure 3-15] The House of Judas Iscariot, reminiscent of Mont Saint-Michel in France

a contradiction to beauty due to the lack of its antagonist". Artworks filled only with elements that have already been defined as beauty, i.e., beauty that has lost any tension with the sublime because it does not contain the potential for the sublime, can no longer be beautiful.[19]

It is rational to believe that such beauty could be attained because there was thorough research on the place and the residents. This is because art that is inappropriate for the place or is disconnected from the living conditions of the residents cannot help but be kitschy. Beauty imposed through the gaze of the other, i.e., artwork that is presented as 'accept this as art', is prone to be filled only with 'elements defined as beauty'. If the textuality of the place and the life of the residents made public art not kitsch but art, the 12 small church buildings, along with several islands, are more than deserving of the honor of sparkling beauty.

Park Kyung-il, a reporter for the Korean newspaper MunhwaIlbo, offered this review after visiting Seomtiago: "What is astonishing about the architecture of these chapels is that they go beyond their own beauty and give elasticity and tension to the entire landscape of the island."[20]

Maintaining tension within the harmony of nature and architecture, that is beauty.

The islands that make up Gijeom-Soakdo island are connected by a causeway that links the islands twice a day at low tide. The causeway is a low bridge made by island residents who wanted to walk between the islands, throwing stones to form it. It's a structure filled with the desperate hope of residents who wanted to escape their solitude. The causeway, which creates a miraculous spectacle worthy of being called the 'Korean version of Moses' Miracle', is said to be as long as 2km when combined with the Byeongpungdo island road and Sinchudo island. The tidal flats around Gijom-Soakdo island have high ecological conservation value, so much so that they have been designated as a UNESCO Biosphere Reserve, a Ramsar Wetland, and a Tidal Flat Provincial Park. The domestic and foreign artists who participated in the creation reportedly interacted informally with the villagers. They utilized many tools available on the island in their works, and the 8th chapel, although resembling the Russian Orthodox Church, embodied the island's specialty product, onions. The 10th chapel used to be a dump where old fishing gear piled up and stench was severe, but the surrounding area was cleaned up with the installation of the chapel building. The development of tourist resources has also led to the improvement of the island's environment, so the residents can't help but welcome it.

5. The Ongoing 'One Museum Per One Island Project' in Shinan County

Could the "One Museum Per One Island Project", which is attracting a line of world-class artists and their works, potentially overlook local identity? Lee Seung-mi, the director of the Evening Glow Art Museum, diagnosed that the "One Museum Per One island Project" will succeed when local art and global art are well combined. She argues that the "One Museum Per One island Project" is fundamentally a regional vitality project that prevents 'desolation', and that global art and local art should proceed on two tracks. She hoped to attract audiences with global art, and to have them encounter and be moved by local art while traveling around the area.

In this context, what Director Lee is interested in is the East Asia Human Rights Peace Museum in Sinuido island, which will primarily exhibit the works of Hong Sung-dam, a folk artist from Shinan. Hong Sung-dam is an artist who devoted himself to printmaking closely related to the spirit of the times, participating directly in the May 18th Democratization Movement that took place in 1980. He pioneered the world of participatory art by forming the 'National Folk Art Movement Alliance (Minmiyeon)' and drawing a series of hanging pictures called 〈National Liberation Movement History〉 with other artists. Director Lee said she expects the museum to serve as a global platform displaying the works of East Asian folk artists, although Hong Sung-dam's folk art will be the main focus.

An archive hall of Korean political history is set to be built in Hauido island, the hometown of former President Kim Dae-jung, a Nobel Peace Prize laureate. It will highlight the long journey of democratization through photographs capturing representative moments in Korean political history. The Cheonsa(Angel) Statue Art Museum has already been established in Hauido. 318 angel statues ranging from 50cm to 3m in height, along with three commemorative sculptures, have been installed throughout Hauido island. The entire Hauido island has been transformed into an Cheonsa(Angel) Park, an open-air museum, attracting visitors' attention along with other local attractions such as the birthplace of President Kim Dae-jung and the large rock face. Former President Kim Dae-jung is indeed a prominent global politician produced by Shinan.

A cultural facility designed by world-renowned installation artist Olafur Eliasson will be established on Dochodo island. Eliasson is an artist who received critical acclaim for his 'Weather Project' at the Tate Modern in London, which involved creating a massive sun with 200 low-pressure sodium lamps. He has installed his works in major cities around the world. The cultural facility of the earth, which will be built at the very top of the Hydrangea Park, past a forest made up of pine trees brought from all over the country, is expected to serve as an observatory that overlooks the surroundings.

On Imjado island, which is connected to the mainland by Yeonryuk Bridge (e.g., connecting bridge between mainland and island), the Woobong Cho Hee-ryong Art Museum has been completed. It exhibits various records about island culture that Cho Hee-ryong, a late Joseon Dynasty painter who was exiled to Imjado island and lived there for three years, experienced on the island, along with the works he left on Imjado island and his life. Works by Lee Lee-nam, one of the best media artists in Korea, are installed along with Woobong's red plum blossom paintings.

In Jido-eup, an embroidery museum is planned to be built to exhibit the works of Imi Ryeo, a master of embroidery culture and art, and pass down her techniques. The Shinan Mudflat Museum has already been built next to the Eldorado Resort. The Infinito Museum, which will soon be completed on Jaeundo island, is operating alongside the 1004 island Stone Art Museum and the World Shell Museum. With improved accessibility due to the construction of an airport, Heuksando island is home to a private art museum by Oriental painter Park Deuk-soon, a bird museum, and a new craft museum. The Jangsando White Museum has been completed on Jangsando, which exhibits works by artists such as painters and calligraphers from Jangsando. The World Fossil and Mineral Museum has been completed on Anjwado island, and the Eros Calligraphy Museum is being operated by remodeling a closed school in Sinseok-ri, Amtae-myeon.

Lastly, the Evening Glow Art Museum, located in Aphae-eup with a superb sea view, is permanently exhibiting the works of Wooam Park Yong-gyu. Lee Seung-mi, the director of the Evening Glow Art Museum located in Aphaedo island, where the islands of Shinan begin, anticipated that the museum will play a central museum role in the "One Museum Per One Island Project". It is expected to take on a key central role, such as synthesizing the contents displayed in 24 museums or rotating exhibits. The Yellow Sea Exchange History Museum and the Intangible Cultural Heritage Center, which will exhibit over 20,000 relics of Shinan Treasure island, will be built on Aphaedo island.

Shinan county expects the "One Museum Per One Island Project" to generate 260.5 billion won in production-inducing effects, 110.2 billion won in value-added effects, and 3,386 jobs. However, the ripple effect of establishing a concentration of museums without precedent worldwide is expected to be unimaginably large. It will claim a place as a new art island entirely different from Naoshima in Japan.

Here Comes The Purple Island

Chapter 4
For the Place Marketing Strategy of Shinan County

Kim Byoung Hee(Seowon University)

Shinan county is carrying out place marketing activities in various areas, including Banwol-Bakjido island, Gijeom-Soakdo island, Seondo island, Uido island, Jangdo island, Imjado island, Bigeumdo island, Dochodo island, Heuksando island, Sinuido island, Aphaedo island, and Jaeundo island. Place marketing is a variety of marketing activities that commodify a unique image to establish a specific region or place as an attractive location, thereby increasing profits and creating added value. Many local governments are universally pursuing policies that seek to revitalize the local economy by utilizing the unique characteristics of a place.

Launching place marketing activities can establish the identity of the area, improve the quality of life of local residents, and attract tourists. Since place marketing affects the formation of a positive perception about a certain area, it is widely utilized when developing tourist sites or attractions. In this chapter, we will examine the concept and characteristics of place marketing, review examples of place marketing, and present the place marketing strategy needed for Shinan county by analyzing the examples of place marketing in Shinan county.

1. Concept and Characteristics of Place Marketing

With the advent of the era of local autonomy in 1995, local governments nationwide began to carry out place marketing activities in the process of seeking regional development strategies to attract companies and visitors. The term city marketing emerged in the 1970s in the United States during the process of redeveloping the city center to develop and manage the city. Local governments in Korea attempted to sell cities or places like products while conducting city marketing activities as a way to revitalize the local economy.

However, city marketing is a sub-concept of place marketing. In Europe, the term "place marketing" was first used in the 1980s to expand the achievements of urban redevelopment projects in the United States. Place marketing refers to various marketing activities aimed at making a certain place known, with the purpose of making the entities managing the place perceived as attractive to residents and tourists.[1] Therefore, place marketing inevitably attracts the interest of policy makers involved in urban planning and local governments around the world facing global competition.

Local governments in our country also tried to consolidate public sentiment and establish the identity of the region through place marketing activities. Local governments attempted to sell the region's places to attract capital and draw in visitors and immigrants. They often engaged in place marketing activities utilizing festivals or cultural and artistic contents. The phenomenon of local governments competing with each other to promote regional festivals also intensified. Both residents of each region and local governments strove to build cooperative relationships to create shared values. These efforts by local governments contributed to fostering a sense of community among local residents and improving life satisfaction.

Public servants of local governments typically understand

all local development strategies implemented to attract capital and manpower and revitalize the local economy using the socio-cultural characteristics of a place as place marketing activities. Ultimately, place marketing as perceived by local governments is marketing activity to sell the image of a place to inform residents, tourists, and businesses that the region is an attractive place. Therefore, a public-private partnership is essential to revitalize the local economy by launching place marketing activities.

So, what are the characteristics of place marketing, which involves various participants? The interactions among participating entities and the supporting institutions and environments have a significant impact on the policy processes of local governments. Competing between local governments based on the unique assets of the region is akin to territorial competition over a particular place. That is, the characteristic of place marketing lies in securing a competitive advantage by forming different features of a place differently from other regions.

In order to survive the competition between regions and develop the local area, local governments conduct place marketing activities considering the assets and characteristics of the region. Among the assets of the region, cultural assets are particularly important. Types of place marketing are classified into cultural place marketing targeting tourists, ecological place marketing, and industrial place marketing for attracting companies. In addition, depending on the approach, place marketing is classified into an integrated model, cultural industry model, and consumer-oriented model.

There are two rules according to the characteristics for place marketing to activate the local tourism industry. There is a hardware method, such as developing tourist spots or building film shooting sets, and a software method, such as planning local festivals, eco-tourism, and green tourism, or developing cultural and artistic content. In order to succeed in place marketing, institutional thickness, where organizations related to creating innovation are gathered in a specific space or region, is particularly important. This means that associated organizations, such as residents, companies, and local governments, must be gathered in one place. Furthermore, it means that all related organizations need to build a consensus of interaction based on mutual trust that tasks are performed together.[2]

The concrete results of place marketing can be evaluated to some extent depending on the achievement of the external purpose of revitalizing the local economy by increasing visitors and the internal purpose of developing local culture and fostering a sense of community among residents. To carry out place marketing activities, it is necessary to first attempt to make a place in a certain area that you want to announce, and in this process, the unique charm of a certain place is formed. The process of actively informing the assets of a certain place to residents, tourists, and companies, and reflecting the results back into the promotion and formation of place assets is repeated, thus completing the place marketing activities.[3] As the place as a product is the sum of the facilities and convenience provided there, there are considerable differences in the approach from general product marketing.

2. Cases of Place Marketing

Researchers have illuminated the value of place

marketing from various perspectives over time. It's interesting to see the study results that evaluated place marketing activities as useful in securing Incheon's local identity and revitalizing the local economy. This study reported that the factor of reliability had the greatest influence on inducing citizens' spontaneity compared to other factors such as mutual control, satisfaction, relationships of coexistence, citizen contribution, intimacy, and community relations.[4] Furthermore, it presented five practical strategies as place marketing measures to enhance Incheon's city image, such as strategies utilizing cultural heritage, cultural events, films, sports, and CI, which would also be useful if applied to the place marketing activities of Shinan county.

The case study of Westergasfabriek (WGF), a residential and commercial area in Amsterdam, the Netherlands, is also worth noting. Westergasfabriek Park in Amsterdam is a case of space reuse. The Westergasfabriek factory located on the outskirts of Amsterdam was built in 1885. It produced fuel for streetlights that lit up the city by extracting gas from coal, but eventually ceased operation as the price competitiveness of gas decreased. In 2003, the city of Amsterdam conducted an urban regeneration project centered on the factory building. Several buildings on the factory site were transformed into large cultural spaces, shops, restaurants, art galleries, etc., and the gas factory, which had lost its function, was transformed into a rest and cultural space for citizens. Witte de Withstraat (WdW), the second city in the Netherlands and the largest port city in Europe, has transformed into a street full of free-spirited and colorful artists. Witte de Withstraat is about 500 meters connecting the downtown of Rotterdam and Museum Park. It is known as the street of artists with various galleries and art institutions gathered, and it is a place exuding a unique freewheeling and individuality with unique shops, cafes, restaurants, and bars. The study that analyzed the creative management strategies of the two places evaluated that as a result of combining various cultural activity elements, the two places were transformed into attractive places, and such results appeared because they understood socio-cultural drivers and carried out place marketing activities.[5)]

In a study analyzing the distribution and attributes of ecotourism resources in Shinan county, it was reported that due to the characteristics of the islands, there are abundant natural ecotourism resources compared to the inland areas, and many unique historical and cultural resources of Shinan county are distributed. Looking at the pattern of the distribution of ecotourism destinations in Shinan county, it is mainly distributed in coastal areas due to the characteristics of the island area. This study presented a vivid and concrete aspect of the ecotourism resources in Shinan county by categorizing the ecotourism resources of Shinan county into natural tourism resources, historical and cultural tourism resources, facility and place tourism resources, and mudflat experience tourism resources, and then subdividing them.[6)]

There are various means necessary for conducting place marketing activities. Among various means, the hosting of exhibitions is often utilized. Local governments hold exhibitions to improve systems and facilities in the direction preferred by residents, visitors, and business personnel, thereby enhancing the value of a certain place. Holding an exhibition to maximize marketing effects at a relatively low cost is also an effective means of place marketing.

Similarly, in Shinan county, a systematic plan for place marketing should be established to set Shinan county as a valuable regional brand and to promote Shinan county and Purple island by specifying 'what', 'to whom', 'why', and 'how' to select various media among various local governments. You can check the progression steps necessary for conducting place marketing activities in Shinan county using exhibitions. When deploying place marketing strategies through exhibitions, it is necessary to consider four stages: research stage, strategy formulation stage, execution stage, and adjustment control stage.

3. Place Marketing Strategy of Shinan County

The place marketing strategy and measures for Shinan county can be prepared from various angles depending on the approach. Nevertheless, the place marketing strategy that urgently needs to be promoted at the current stage can be summarized into six main categories. First, Shinan county needs to carry out integrated marketing communication activities; second, it needs to establish tourism branding for Purple island; third, it needs to explore the diverse functions of art galleries and museums planned in Shinan county. Fourth, it needs to operate village autonomous activities in Shinan county; fifth, it needs to develop global marketing programs; and sixth, it needs to conduct reciprocal patron activities. The place marketing strategy and implementation measures of Shinan county can be explained in more detail as follows:

1) Deployment of Integrated Marketing Communication

Integrated Marketing Communication (IMC) targets various stakeholder groups, considers various communication areas, considers all brand contact points, influences specific sales behavior, and ultimately aims to build relationships with customers.

Therefore, marketers need to change their perception of marketing from the 4P (product, price, distribution, promotion) concept to the 4C (customer, cost, convenience, communication) concept in order to build relationships with customers or visitors. In other words, they need to research what customers want and need rather than the product itself, understand the cost customers pay to satisfy their desires rather than the price, consider the convenience of the purchase process rather than the place of purchase, and focus on communication with customers rather than promotion efforts.

For example, in the case of Shinan county, they need to study the needs of visitors rather than overly emphasizing the superiority of Shinan county and Purple island (product → consumer), and consider the cost visitors pay to visit Purple island rather than overly adhering to the value of Shinan county and Purple island (price → cost). Moreover, they should highlight the convenience of Shinan county and Purple island rather than focusing on the places themselves (place → convenience), and they should prioritize communication with visitors rather than focusing too much on promotion activities (promotion → communication).

Especially, in order to continuously improve the recognition of Shinan county and Purple island, a strategy and tactics for building trust with current and potential customers must be urgently established. Trust has the greatest impact on the formation of civic relationships. The overall and integrated planning ability influences the improvement of recognition of Shinan county and Purple island more than any single context. When deploying place marketing, it is necessary to continuously communicate according to visitors' knowledge and tastes, and by providing various programs, the recognition of Shinan county and Purple island can continue to increase.

An important point not to be missed in the place marketing strategy of Shinan county is the need to normalize and diversify communication contact points. Integrated Marketing Communication recommends considering all brand contact points for any brand to succeed. If Shinan county wants to succeed in the place marketing strategy in the future, it must consider various communication areas for various stakeholder groups and consider Shinan county's brand contact points that can influence specific behavioral responses of visitors. In order to spread interest in Shinan county nationwide, place marketing activities must be carried out nationwide. The future place marketing activities of Shinan county should not be a temporary sparkling method centered on Purple island, but should build a continuous relationship between Shinan county and visitors by allowing visitors to frequently come into contact with the brand of Shinan county in their daily lives.

2) Establishment of Tourism Branding for Purple island

Establishing a tourism branding strategy for Purple island in a long-term context is an urgent task facing Shinan county. In other words, a unique place image needs to be built in the long term by connecting the entire Shinan county centered on the place called Purple island. It is necessary to plan events that can form brand assets, provide residential value and investment value in modern meaning, form a tourist belt linking various places, develop brand slogans, and plan festival events centered on citizens.

For a place to grow into a noteworthy region, it must have visitability, livability, and investability. There are certain limits to continuously attracting tourists just by emphasizing the purple color of Purple island, and it is difficult to meet the needs and desires of tourists. Therefore, to make Shinan county a more noticed island, various modern events themed around Purple island should be planned, and exploratory trips or experiential programs should be developed to increase visitability and build an image of a place where people want to invest.

Shinan county has achieved some results by deploying place marketing for Purple island using purple, but in the future, more strategic color marketing activities need to be deployed. Through a linkage strategy with other local governments, Purple island should be established as a nationwide tourist attraction. According to the principles of cultural branding, for a brand to become a strong brand, it needs to expand the meaning of the brand and build an iconic brand image. In this regard, the color marketing activities of Shinan county are a beneficial plan to expand the meaning of the Purple island brand.

In a study examining the tourism marketing strategy of local governments centered on Asan City, Chungnam, it was stated that in order for Asan City to grow into a famous tourist spot, it needs to strengthen its strengths as a place where you can have short-term tours with convenient transportation, and a place where you can explore history and enjoy nature-friendly and hot spring relaxation. To compensate for the weaknesses, it was suggested to develop slogans to create a distinctive image and strengthen the tourism administration system and marketing activities.[7] The way to compensate for weaknesses is also worth referring to in the place marketing activities of Shinan county. To activate the tourism industry of Shinan county, it is necessary to consider the place marketing strategy model.

3) Diversified Function Exploration of Art Museums and Museums

To revitalize tourism in Shinan county, we should actively explore ways to establish and revitalize art museums and museums on various islands in Shinan county. Under the premise that there are limits to mobilizing viewers in traditional ways, the opinions of experts should be used as important reference materials in establishing and operating art museums and museums. And we need to be more proactive in promoting policies to invite world-renowned artists to Shinan. It is also desirable to provide them with a workspace while exhibiting their works. Along with them, we need to plan high-quality exhibitions and operate virtual galleries online, and develop cultural content related to Shinan county.

Shinan county promoted the "One Museum Per One Island Project" to enhance the cultural pride of island residents, increase opportunities for cultural enjoyment, and revitalize the region using culture and art. The plan is to build a total of 25 cultural and artistic spaces, including 9 museums, 10 art galleries, 3 exhibition halls, and 3 parks, and 14 have already been completed and are welcoming visitors. More specifically, the 14 places include ① Aphaedo Evening Glow Art Museum, ② Jeungdo Shinan Mudflat Museum, ③ Jaeundo 1004 Island Rock Art Museum, ④ Jaeundo World Shellfish Museum, ⑤ Bigeumdo Lee Se-dol Baduk Museum, ⑥ Heuksando Bak Deuk-soon Art Museum, ⑦ Heuksando Bird Museum, ⑧ Heuksando Bird Craft Museum, ⑨ Hauido Cheonsa (Angel) Statue Art Museum, ⑩ Anjwado World Fossil Mineral Museum, ⑪ Amtaedo Eros Calligraphy Museum, ⑫ Imjado Cho Hee-ryong Art Museum, ⑬ Shinan Native Plant Research Center, ⑭ Jangsando White Museum. And the 11 places including ① Aphaedo Yellow Sea Exchange History Museum, ② Aphaedo Intangible Cultural Heritage Center, ③ Jaeundo Infinito Museum (Shinan County Art Museum), ④ Bigeumdo Sea Culture Facility, ⑤ Dochodo Earth Culture

Facility, ⑥ Hauido Republic of Korea Political History Archive Hall, ⑦ Sinuido East Asia Human Rights Peace Museum, ⑧ Anjwado Floating Art Museum, ⑨ Sinuido Korea Chunran Museum, ⑩ Jido Embroidery Museum, ⑪ Jaeundo Complex Culture Tourism Town are targets of the art project.

This attempt is consistent with the recommendation of marketing expert Philip Kotler, which emphasizes the need to strengthen the market-oriented perspective among marketing measures of cultural and artistic institutions. In the future, Shinan county should actively use cultural marketing strategies necessary for attracting visitors by developing various cultural programs within the art museum, rather than emphasizing only the unique exhibition function of the art museum. Furthermore, programs that can provide meaningful visit experiences to visitors need to be developed from various perspectives.

4) Operation of Village Autonomy Activities in Shinan County

Village autonomy activities of residents in Shinan county

will also help to apply place marketing activities to reality. Thomas Jefferson, the third President of the United States, claimed that the future of the entire republic lies in the construction of a village republic and named the village government, where villagers directly participate and solve village problems, as the elementary republic. Based on the logic that true democracy extends to the whole when such village republics gather, he argued that the size of the village should be small enough for all residents to directly participate, and large enough to properly perform village tasks. This is the core concept of the village republic and the elementary republic that Jefferson argued.

Gandhi, a great leader of India, envisioned and propagated village autonomy for true independence throughout his life. For Gandhi, the village was an independent autonomous republic. Gandhi said, arguing that the federation should function to connect village republics, and that all functions of the state should essentially be in the village, "The village is the smallest political unit with the most complete power, so every individual can directly voice. Each individual is an architect who establishes his or her own government." Even in India, which is slower in economic development compared to our country, the revised "Constitution" of 1993 guaranteed the village autonomy proposed by Gandhi to a considerable extent.[8]

In the future, village autonomy activities in Shinan county need to establish the direction of village autonomy through the concretization of pillar. The pillar, meaning a column, refers to the sub-concept that specifically supports to achieve a certain concept and goal. For example, if the theme is a higher concept in storytelling, the detailed elements necessary to complete the theme, such as plot, material, and protagonist, are pillars. We can think of SMILE as a brand to inform Shinan county's village autonomy. SMILE means 'building a village by oneself' in Korean, which is an acronym created by taking the first syllable of three words.

Let's elaborate more specifically on the brand concept of SMILE, an integrated brand for village autonomy. That is, a Safe village, a Mind-full village filled with a sharing spirit, an Impressive village with plenty of memorable memories and opportunities, a Linked village growing through solidarity and sharing, and an Emotional village full of emotional vitality. These five concepts concretely express the meaning of safety, solidarity, and vitality. Village autonomy in each region of Shinan county can only be completed when local residents and policy stakeholders communicate and participate with each other to realize true governance.

In order to support SMILE, the village autonomy activities of residents in Shinan county, five principles must be consistently adhered to. Policy officials in Shinan county need to divide the image of a village made by the residents themselves into five areas and convey specific principles to the residents. The first principle is the 'arm's length' principle of support but non-interference (Support-noninterference principle) in Shinan county, and the second principle is the principle of evaluating according to performance rather than evenly distributing the budget (More and more principle). The third principle is the principle of integrating from individual village autonomy to the entire village autonomy of Shinan county (Integrated principle), and the fourth principle is the principle of aiming for a long-term campaign rather than focusing on short-term results (Long-term campaign principle). The last, fifth principle is the ESG principle that values and aims for the environment, society, and governance (ESG oriented principle).

5) Development of Global Marketing Program

The development of a global marketing program to widely publicize Shinan county around the world must also be prepared in a concrete and realistic context. Global marketing is a marketing activity targeting more than two countries in order to achieve marketing purposes. To mark Shinan county as an impressive place in the hearts of people around the world, it is necessary to select only the advantages of various fields such as content marketing, place marketing, culture and art marketing, and tourism marketing, and to adapt them to the reality of Shinan county.

For example, there could be various ideas such as developing courses for foreigners, building digital-based international networks, and holding international exhibitions. The creation of value in the cultural industry can secure competitiveness at home and abroad by reinforcing management assets such as planning ability and marketing power. To promote Shinan county globally, we need to avoid event-oriented planning and develop global programs based on systematic and sustainable execution plans. Based on a concrete execution plan, Shinan county should enhance its awareness and preference, and at the same time establish an image of a remarkable place beyond the character of a simple tourist spot.

For instance, the sculpture of The Little Prince installed in Banwoldo island in Shinan county also symbolizes the 'dream of innocence.' The Little Prince (1943), a fairy tale that everyone has read at least once, is written by Antoine de Saint-Exupéry, a French airplane pilot and novelist. After the first edition was published, more than 450 translated editions were released, and it is a global steady seller that has sold over 200 million copies so far. If Shinan county and Nice, a resort city in France, become sister cities through the sculpture of The Little Prince and exchange tourism programs, it will be a good example of promoting a global marketing program from the standpoint of Shinan county.

In April 2021, the resort city of Nice, France, installed an

[Figure 4-1] **Sculpture of The Little Prince in Banwoldo island**

out of home advertising monument on the promenade of Nice beach to commemorate the 75th anniversary of the first publication of "The Little Prince" and to remember novelist Antoine de Saint-Exupery.[9] Nice, one of the top resort cities in France, is a city loved by artists such as Matisse and Chagall, located on the Mediterranean Sea, close to the Principality of Monaco and Italy. Nice, included in the Côte d'Azur region, extends to Monaco and Cannes, and the cobalt coast of the Mediterranean is endlessly filled with luxurious hotels and villas.

Saint-Exupéry married his wife Consuelo at Nice City Hall in 1931 and lived in Nice for several years after marriage. The name of the wedding hall at Nice City Hall was recently changed to 'Saint-Exupery Consuelo'. Saint-Exupéry showed us what true happiness is through the questions of The Little Prince. The outdoor advertising monument includes various props, including the illustration of The Little Prince drawn by the author in "The Little Prince". The phrase "I Love NICE" on the outdoor advertisement reminds us of the slogan "I Love NY" of New York City, USA, but it contains the heart of Saint-Exupéry, who loved Nice. Plus, the number 75 was perfect for commemorating the 75th anniversary of the publication of "The Little Prince".

Depending on the person, "The Little Prince" can be read from various angles, but the true theme of this book is to find true happiness for a 'better self.'[10] Tourists from our country who have looked at the sculpture of The Little Prince in Banwoldo island, as well as tourists from Nice, France, who came to see Purple island, will be immersed in the 'dream of innocence'. Wouldn't they think about what

[Figure 4-2] Out of home advertising monument for the 75th anniversary of "The Little Prince" (2021)

true happiness is, following the famous quote from the fairy tale?

> "If you come at four in the afternoon, I shall begin to be happy by three."
>
> "Draw me a sheep."
>
> "What is essential is invisible to the eye."
>
> "One must reserve one's words of love."

"The most difficult task in the world is to win a person's heart."
"Stars are beautiful because of a flower that cannot be seen."
"The desert is beautiful because it hides a well somewhere."
"It is the time you have wasted for your rose that makes your rose so important."
"All grown-ups were once children... but only few of them remember it."

6) Expansion of Mutually Beneficial Philanthropy Activities

Policy officials in Shinan county should actively explore ways to raise funds for activating tourism in Shinan county and Purple island. Fundraising is a critical strategy in place marketing, so it should be incorporated into the place marketing strategy of Shinan county and Purple island. From the perspective of seeking a win-win strategy with corporations, Shinan county needs to actively expand corporate philanthropy activities.

Mecenat is a French term that collectively refers to the act of corporations returning their profits to society and supporting the field of arts and culture. The ancient Roman politician, Gaius Clinius Maecenas, who loved art, maintained a close relationship with contemporary poets like Horace and Virgil and supported their creative activities. The term mecenat is derived from his name. In advanced countries such as the United States, Europe, and Japan, corporate members have long established Mecenat Councils to support their country's cultural and artistic activities. Recently, they have been expanding their support to various public interest fields such as sports activities, social projects, and humanitarian projects. In South Korea, the Korea Corporate Philanthropy Association (www. mecenat.or.kr) has been operating as a non-profit corporation since April 18, 1994.

Moving forward, Shinan county should consider launching profit-making businesses or partnering with media companies to carry out nationwide fundraising campaigns. Shinan county should establish a mecenat strategy targeting the central government, local governments, media companies, corporations, and individuals based on the contents they possess. In this process, they need to find ideas that can provide mutual benefits. It is crucial to disseminate the content of Shinan county and Purple island domestically and internationally, positioning them as objects of affection. Furthermore, they need to develop tourism products and carry out place marketing activities to induce synergy effects with the sponsor groups.

End Note

Chapter 1 Color Marketing that Attracts People

1 Kim Byoung-hee (July 13, 2023). "Color Marketing for Shinan County's Purple Island, which Rejected the Age of Population Extinction." *Korea Economic Daily*. https://www.hankyung.com/article/2023071219911

2 Kim Myung-won (March 29, 2022). "Color Marketing that Moves People's Hearts." *Consumer Evaluation*. http://www.iconsumer.or.kr/news/articleView.html?idxno=23870

3 Lee Young-ju, & Jo Dong-hyuk (2020). "The Effect of Color Marketing on Brand Image, Customer Satisfaction and Revisit Intention." *Journal of Global Business Administration Review, 17*(1), pp. 85-102.

4 Kim Shin-ae, & Kwon Ki-dae (2014). "A Relational Analysis among Color Marketing, Brand Charisma and Marketing Outcome." *Journal of the Korea Academia-Industrial Cooperation Society, 15*(1), pp. 144-156.

5 Do Ji-yoon, & Seo Ju-hwan (2021). "Analysis of the

Landscape Characteristics of Island Tourist Site Using Big Data: Based on Bakjido and Banwoldo, Shinan County." *Journal of the Korean Institute of Landscape Architecture*, *49*(2), pp. 61-73.

6 Shinan County (2022). "1004 Islands Shinan County Homepage." http://www.shinan.go.kr

7 Shinan County (2022). *Feast of Purple Flowers: Purple Island White Paper*. Jeonnam: Shinan County.

8 The 'Cheonsa Bridge' takes its name from 'Cheonsa', the Korean word for 'angel', which also coincidentally share the same pronunciation with the number 1004, potentially giving a playful or dual meaning to the bridge's name. 1004 is a representative figure for Shinan county which boasts a total of 1004 islands within the region.

9 Tamio Suenaga, translated by Park Pil-im (2001). *Color Psychology*. Seoul: Yekyung.

10 Seth Godin, translated by Nam Soo-young, & Lee Joo-hyung (2004). *Purple Cow*. Seoul: Jaein.

11 Hong Ki-chul (September 1, 2020). "Shinan's Purple Island, the Purple Sanctuary, Became a World Tourist Attraction." *Money S*.

12 Lilit Marcus, & Jake Kwon (February 8, 2021). "South Korea's All-Purple Banwoldo Island is a Photographer's Dream." *CNN*. https://edition.cnn.com/travel/article/banwol-purple-instagram-island-south-korea/index.html

13 Hwang Yoon-jung, & Kim Do-hee (February 23, 2021). "Even Foreign Media Fell in Love: Wonderful! Shinan's

Purple Island." Yonhap News.

14 Shinan County (December 3, 2021). "Purple island, the Best Tourism Village Selected by the UN World Tourism Organization." https://blog.naver.com/1004_shinan/222585873384

15 Shinan County (2022). *Purple Island: A Symphony of Purple Flowers*. Jeonnam: Shinan County.

Chapter 2 Green Marketing that Regenerates Regions with Flowers and Trees

1 Yeo Hun-goo (1995). *Green Marketing*. Seoul: Angraphics. p. 24.

2 Oh Chang-woo (2007). "A Multidimensional Analysis of Green Advertising: A Test of the Nature and Framework of Green Appeals." *Korean Journal of Advertising, 18*(1), pp. 7-39.

3 Kilbourne, W. E. (1995). "Green Advertising: Salvation or Oxymoron?" *Journal of Advertising, 24*(2), pp. 7-19.

4 Lee Sang-seon (August 10, 2022). "10-Ri Forest of Pine Trees: Shinan County Takes the Lead in Carbon Neutrality." *Gwangju Daily*.

5 Kyuhoshi Japan Travel & Culture Guide (July 7, 2022). "10 Best Flower Fields in Hokkaido." https://www.kyuhoshi.com/best-flower-fields-in-hokkaido/

6 'Ri' is a traditional Korean unit of distance measurement. For reference, 10-ri is equivalent to approximately 4 kilometers.

7 Lee Jae-eon (April 30, 2021). *Islands of Korea*. Jeonnam: Shinan County.

8 Hong Kyung-soo, Professor, Department of Culture and Content, Ajou University.

9 'Pyeong' is a traditional Korean unit of area measurement. One pyeong is approximately equivalent to 3.3 square meters or 35.5 square feet.

10 Lee Jae-jin (March 14, 2022). "Seondo Narcissus Festival, a Luxury Narcissus island in a Flower Garden Planted by island Grandmothers." *Monthly San*. http://san.chosun.com/news/articleView.html?idxno=15632

11 Jung Heon-gwan (2008). *Trees in Our Life*. Seoul: Eomungak.

12 Kim Kyung-ok (July 1, 2021). "Jeonnam Hope Icon island · Sea Story: Hydrangea Heaven Shinan Dochodo island." *Namdo Daily*.http://www.namdonews.com/news/articleView.html?idxno=651811

13 Monthly San (May 13, 2021). "Shinan Special Feature: Hydrangeas are Blooming, Summer is Just Around the Corner." *Monthly San*.

14 Kim Kyung-ok (July 1, 2021). "Jeonnam Hope Icon island · Sea Story: Hydrangea Heaven Shinan Dochodo island." *Namdo Daily*.http://www.namdonews.com/news/articleView.html?idxno=651811

15 HankookIlbo (October 19, 2021). "700 Pine Trees in Danger Moved to This island to Become a Premium Forest." *HankookIlbo*. https://www.hankookilbo.com/News/Read/

A20211019092200001640?did=NA

16 Jung Yong-sik (January 11, 2021). "Shinan County's Aphedo and Bonsai Park Camellia." *Herald Economy*. http://news.heraldcorp.com/view.php?ud=20210111000942

17 Monthly San (January 3, 2020). "1004 islands Shinan Special Feature: Aphedo Winter Flower Festival, New Camellia Spot Aphedo Bonsai Park." *Monthly San*. http://san.chosun.com/news/articleView.html?idxno=13416

18 Kim Jun (May 17, 2019). "When the Heart Opens, the Sea Route Opens, Goheung County, Jeonnam Sook island." *Republic of Korea Policy Briefing*. https://www.korea.kr/news/cultureColumnView.do?newsId=148860941

19 Ko Seung-chan (May 28, 2020). "Selection of olive varieties for open-field cultivation to create new income sources." *New Jeju Daily*. http://www.jejuilbo.net/news/articleView.html?idxno=145534

20 Hong Seon-gi (2019). *Island Studies*. Seoul: Folklore Institute.

Chapter 3 Art Marketing that Revives a Region with Art

1 JTBC (June 9, 2021). "Art Thieves." *JTBC*.

2 Shinan County (2022). "County Collection Art." https://www.shinan.go.kr/home/www/about/cultural/cultural_art/collection_01/page.wscms

3 Kim Whan-ki (2005). *Where and What to Meet Again*. Seoul: Whan-ki Art Museum. p. 30.

4 Kim Whan-ki (2005). Ibid. p. 113.

5 Kim Whan-ki (2005). Ibid. pp. 131-132.

6 Kim Whan-ki (2005). Ibid. pp. 216-217.

7 Kim Whan-ki (2005). Ibid. p. 211.

8 Lee Young-ran (June 29, 2022). "The sculpture of Park Eun-sun will stand tall on Bocelli's stage, Infinite Column." *NewsPim*. https://www.newspim.com/news/view/20220629000837

9 MARIO BOTTA STUDIO (2022). http://www.botta.ch/en/STUDIO

10 Mario Botta, in an interview at the Leeum Museum.

11 From the movie "Mario Botta: Architecture for the Soul."

12 Lim Narae (November 6, 2021). "Gallery on the Street: The architectural work left in Korea by Mario Botta, the synonym of red brick." *Culture News*. http://www.mhns.co.kr/news/articleView.html?idxno=515044

13 Choi Sun-hee (May 15, 2011). "When the freedom of the body is limited, the human soul goes further." *JoongAng Sunday*. https://www.joongang.co.kr/article/5488187

14 Choi Sun-hee (May 15, 2011). "When the freedom of the body is limited, the human soul goes further." *JoongAng Sunday*. https://www.joongang.co.kr/article/5488187

15 Choi Sun-hee (May 15, 2011). "When the freedom of the body is limited, the human soul goes further." *JoongAng Sunday*. https://www.joongang.co.kr/article/5488187

16 Rebecca Solnit, translated by Kim Jeong-ah (2017). *A Field Guide to Getting Lost*. Seoul: Half Empty. p. 20. (Modified by the author).

17 'Seomtiago' is a clever wordplay inspired by the famous Spanish pilgrimage, 'El Camino de Santiago.' By substituting 'San' in 'Santiago' with 'Seom' (Korean for 'island'), it highlights both the iconic Spanish trail and Shinan County's island-centric religious attractions.

18 Son Sang-won (September 2, 2018). "Designing an island: Yoon Mi-sook, Jeonnam Province island Expert Committee." *Yonhap News*.

19 Seo Young-chae (2013). *Concept Garden of Humanities*. Seoul: Moonji. p. 192.

20 Park Kyung-il (October 11, 2019). "Walking the 'Little Santiago,' a Healing Road Connecting Four islands." *MunhwaIlbo*.

Chapter 4 For the Place Marketing Strategy of Shinan County

1 Kearns, G., & Philo, C. (1993). "Culture, History, Capital: A critical introduction to the Selling." In G. Kearns & C. Philo (Eds.). *Selling Places: The City as Cultural Capital and Past and Present*. Oxford: Pergamon Press.

2 Kim Hyung-gook (2002). *The Cultural Promotion of Hometown: The Way for the Local to Survive in the Era of Globalization*. Seoul: Hakgojae.

3 Kim Hyun-ho (2003). "Place Asset Making in Place Marketing for Regional Development." *Land Research, 36*, pp. 77-95.

4 Lee, Soo-beom (2004). "Place Marketing Strategy for Enhancing City Image: Focused on Incheon." *Communication Studies, 12*(1), pp. 56-83.

5 Hitters, E., & Richards, G. (2002). "The Creation and Management of Cultural Clusters." *Creativity and Innovation Management, 11*(4), pp. 234-247.

6 Gu Ho, & Kim Nong-o (2009). "A Study on the Suitability Analysis for Shinangun Eco-Tourism Area." *Korea Tourism Research Association, 23*(1), pp. 267-278.

7 Lee In-gu (2010). "A Study on IMC Approach to Tourism Marketing Communication Strategies of Local Government: Focused on A-San City in Chungcheongnamdo." *Korean Journal of Photo-Geography, 20*(4), pp. 139-151.

8 JoongAngIlbo (September 30, 2019). "Lee Ki-woo's Perspective: We Need to Introduce Proper Village Autonomy Instead of the Mere Form of Resident Autonomy." *JoongAngIlbo*.

9 AFP (May 6, 2021). "Love letters and 'The Little Prince'." *AFP*. https://www. globaltimes.cn/page/202105/1222767.shtml

10 Kim Byoung-hee (February 20, 2022). "We Are All the Little Prince in Search of Happiness." Hankyung CMO Insight, *Korea Economic Daily*. https://www.hankyung.com/economy/article/202202205117i

Index

About the Author and Translator

Author

Kim Byoung Hee

Currently serves as a professor in the Department of Advertising and Public Relations at Seowon University. He graduated from Seoul National University and received a Ph.D. in Advertising from Hanyang University. He has served as the 24th President of the Korean Advertising Society, the 15th President of the Korean PR Society, the first Chairman of the Government Advertising Advisory Committee, and the 4th Chairman of the Seoul Brand Committee. He has published over 60 books, including "Sticker Message" (Korea Economic Daily, 2022) and "Cultural Arts Marketing Communication Strategy" (Hakjisa, 2020), and has published over 110 papers on advertising and PR in leading domestic and international journals. His awards include the Grand Prize of the Korean Gallup Academic Prize (2011), the Grand Prize of the first Cheil Worldwide Academic Prize (2012), and the Presidential Commendation (2019) in recognition of his contribution to the government's policy communication. Email: kimthomas@hanmail.net

Hong Kyung Soo

Currently serves as a professor in the Department of Cultural Contents at Ajou University. He graduated from the Department of Journalism and Broadcasting at Korea University, and received his master's and doctoral degrees from the Graduate School of Journalism and Information at Seoul National University. He joined KBS as a PD and first planned "The Discovery of Reading" and "One-Shot Interview," winning the Excellence Award at the Korea Broadcasting Awards. In 2006, he discovered the beauty of Shinan County while producing the Chuseok special documentary "island Village Music Festival," featuring singer Song

Dae-kwan, in Jeungdo island and Uido. He served as a judge for the Baeksang Arts Awards, Korea Broadcasting Awards, and the International Emmy Awards in the U.S., and served as Chairman of the TBS Viewer Committee, KBS Management Evaluation Committee, and Research Director of the Korean Broadcasting Association. His works include "Squid Game and the Content Revolution" (People and Ideas, 2022), "The Humanities of Planning" (Time of the Sea, 2019), "Conversation with an Entertainment PD" (Person, 2016), and his translation "Etymology is Humanities" (Person, 2018). Email: hongks@ajou.ac.kr

Translator

Kim Beom Joo

Currently pursuing a Ph.D. program in Food and Hospitality Systems at the University of Missouri-Columbia. He graduated from Korea University with a bachelor's degree in Geography Education, received a master's degree from the Hospitality Management at the University of Missouri, and is currently completing his Ph.D. program. His main research areas include SMART Tourism, IT Adoption, and Marketing and Consumer Behavior in Hospitality and Tourism field. Some of his notable research papers and conference proceedings include "Effects of source and message on travel YouTube channel: Cognitive and affective destination images of S. Korea," "Exploring the effectiveness of adopting virtual influencer marketing strategy in tourism field," and "Eye-tracking analysis of gain and loss promotion strategy: The interaction effects of product type and price on hotel booking intention." He received the 88th Korea Tourism Association Best Paper Award (2020).
Email: bkqkb@umsystem.edu

Here Comes The Purple Island

A Story of Cultural and Artistic Administration
in the Age of Population Extinction

First edition printed by HAKJISA Publisher on March 1, 2024
First edition published by HAKJISA Publisher on March 5, 2024

Author • Kim Byoung Hee · Hong Kyung Soo
Translator • Kim Beom Joo
Publisher • Kim Jin Hwan
Publishing Company • HAKJISA Publisher, Inc.
Address • Mind World Bldg, 20, Yanghwa-ro 15-gil, Mapo-gu, Seoul 04031, KOREA
Telephone • 02-330-5114 Fax • 02-324-2345
Publisher ID • 313-2006-000265

Homepage • http://www.hakjisa.co.kr
Instagram • https://www.instagram.com/hakjisabook

ISBN 978-89-997-3075-7 03320
List Price • KRW 18,000